Rocking Horses

MARGARET SPENCER

The Crowood Press

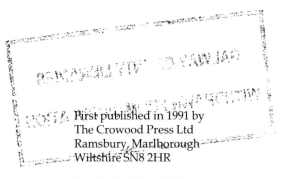

First published in 1991 by
The Crowood Press Ltd
Ramsbury, Marlborough
Wiltshire SN8 2HR

Paperback edition 1998

British Library Cataloguing-in-Publication Data

A catalogue record for this book is available from the British Library.

ISBN 1 86126 182 9

Acknowledgements

The photographs are by Colin Jeffrey and Margaret Spencer

My thanks to:

My husband Ron
My children, Sharon, Peter and Marion
My staff, Victoria, Elizabeth and Nova
Also to Kevin Saunders
For their encouragement, help and patience

Line illustrations by Noël Trimmer

Margaret Spencer
Rocking Horse Specialist
Chard Road
Crewkerne
Somerset TA18 8BA

Typeset by Context, Greenlea House, Green Street, Coopers Hill, Glos GL3 4RT
Printed and bound in Great Britain by WBC Book Manufacturers Ltd, Bridgend

CONTENTS

1	The History of the Rocking Horse	5
2	Getting Started	13
3	Tools	19
4	Accessories	24
5	Medium Horse	36
6	Doll-sized Horse made from Plywood	74
7	Small, Lightly Carved Horse	83
8	Toddlers' Horses	95
9	Large Rocking Horse on Swinger Stand and Rocker	110
10	Restoration	134
11	Tail Piece	159
	Index	160

CHAPTER ONE

THE HISTORY OF THE ROCKING HORSE

From the time when the first horse was tamed, man has loved this splendid creature with its great strength and speed, patience and obedience. Soon it became a status symbol as well as a means of transport and of work, often a companion, and this relationship has stayed the same over the centuries. As soon as life of early man became sophisticated enough to allow the children, especially those of the rich, to have time to play, playthings appeared, and as children love to ape their elders it wasn't long before the hobby-horse evolved. No doubt the first ones were just a stick that the child put between its legs to represent a horse as it galloped along, but hobby-horses became quite complicated affairs quite early on as depicted in ancient paintings from Persia and China. They had elaborately carved heads, manes, reins and wheels at the other end of the pole, very similar to the ones made today.

It is interesting to note that almost all the stages the wooden horse as a toy went through over the centuries, culminating in our present-day rocking horse, are still being made, the hobby-horse being one of the truest examples of this, as it has been continually made since those early days. Jesters throughout the European courts of the Middle Ages used them as a prop for their performances and the old rhyme 'Ride a cock-horse to Banbury Cross' has been with us for generations (cock-horse being another name for hobby-horse).

The first true rocking horse to be seen in Britain appears to be one reputedly brought back from Germany for young Charles I to help him recover from rickets. Whether this tale is true or not no one knows, but Charles I grew up to be a first-class horseman. The Black Forest area of Germany is still noted for the making of rocking horses.

These first rocking horses were very simple, being made up of two semi-circles of oak planking, about the same thickness and breadth as old oak floorboards and 3ft(90cm) long. A rounded log was sandwiched between these two semi-circles to make a seat and another block of wood was carved to make the head, all in oak. A few of this type of horse are still to be found in museums, some with additions of holsters, footrests, backrests and even legs painted on the planking.

From the sixteenth century toy horses developed, capable in the end of carrying children. These were known as barrel horses. The name came from the log-shaped body which was fitted with four pole legs and an outline shape of a horse's head fitted at one end. At first they were only tiny, made of softwood so a small child could carry it under the arm or pull it along on a string, but soon the horse became bigger, but still only about 18in(45cm) high, with the horse's legs fitted into a platform with four small wooden wheels. The child could now sit on the horse and be pulled along. These first barrel horses, because they were made of a softwood, have nearly all disappeared, and are now only to be seen in illustrations, often as incidental background to some more important subject such as a family group.

The reason for the popularity of these barrel horses is very easy to appreciate. Not only were they quick and simple to make, but most of the materials used could be offcuts from other work. The local village carpenter could make this horse as easily as the town cabinet-maker. More important for parent and maker, these toys were very popular with children. On these toys children could sit and copy rich adults. They could let their imaginations run free, even if they themselves were tied to their mother's apron strings. The toy horse was solid and big for a small child and like a real horse it had 'presence'. Moreover other children had them to play with and to share.

The next variation was to provide a handle at the back of the barrel horse. The struts each side of the handle were fixed to the sides of the horse and then went down to where they were slotted into the platform. Now the toddler was able to push the horse as well as ride it, so the toy doubled as a teaching aid when the child was learning to walk. This last variation was a winner, from the time of its appearance in the eighteenth century, when it was called a 'Bristol Toy' and sold in street fairs and markets for one penny. For a time around the turn of the twentieth century the handle struts were iron and sometimes the horse sported mane and tail of horse-hair, but by the 1930s they were back to wooden handle struts and pressed metal wheels with a rubber tyre, while mane and tail were now strips of lamb's wool on the skin. They were so much in demand for toddlers by then that rows and rows would be hung up under the toy shop ceiling.

Alongside the development of the small barrel horse there were also small rocking horses being made. There is not so much documented proof of this, but Benjamin Booth, a turner in London in 1749, advertised his premises as being 'At the sign of the Rocking Horse near Sargeants Inn, Fleet Street'. At the start of the eighteenth century there was an amalgamation of the two types of horse, the rocker and the barrel horse, which meant the barrel horse was much larger and was put on rockers, which were a low curve about 2in(51mm) wide and 1in(25mm) thick, 25in(635mm) long, made of a hardwood, very plain. The horses feet were fitted into 2in(51mm) wide planks which were also the spacer bracing bars for the rockers. The overall height was 27in(686mm). It had a horse-hair mane and tail, there was some shaping to the legs and hooves, the head was quite well shaped with an open mouth to take a bit which was attached to a nailed-on bridle. The horse was painted and had a painted-on saddle on its round barrel body. The measurements for this horse are only approximate as each of these early rocking horses were made individually by such people as carpenters employed on large estates, who would be told that one had to be made for the nursery of the big house.

The development of the rocking horse went on all through the eighteenth century, until by the end they had become beautifully carved, fiery chargers on very deep boat-shaped rockers with curled ends. The horses were shown at full gallop, with heads outstretched, flowing real horse-hair for manes and tails, glass eyes, nailed on leather saddle and bridle. These were known as the Georgian rocking horses. The actual stance of the horse was rather stiff, as shown in hunting and battle scene paintings of the same period. This was because the horse moved so fast the eye was not able to catch all the movements it made. It wasn't until the invention of the movie camera that there was an improvement in depicting horses at full gallop.

The importance, by now, of the rocking horse in the larger nurseries of the aristocracy was shown by the fact that at the base of each side of the neck, just where the saddle begins was a hole for a banana-shaped pummel to be fitted so that the girls could learn to ride side-saddle. Most of the horses were painted a plain colour or white with spots. Young Napoleon of France had a spotted steed. In fact the breed of Appaloosa was very popular at the time until, so the story goes, King George IV was given one as a present by a foreign nobleman. King George gave the horse orders in English, which the horse had never heard before, and therefore, being a very intelligent horse, it thought it had a madman on its back, and threw the King, whereupon King George vowed never to have anything to do with any Appaloosa again. Hence they quickly went out of fashion and so they did for rocking horses. At about the same time it was very fashionable to clip the ears and dock the tails of horses (and dogs) especially those ridden by ladies, hence the ears of the Georgian horses are very small indeed.

Another fashion that was followed from a real horse was around the middle of the nineteenth century the light bearing-rein was used and at about the same time the rocking horses' noses were brought in from the stretched-out position of a full gallop to the dropped-down position of a horse going at a fast trot. This gave rise to them being called jibbers and the Georgian ones were racers. These styles were universally accepted by 1850, so too was the method of construction. Andrew Mayhew wrote a number of articles for the *Morning Chronicle* and in one, dated 21 February of that year, he concentrates upon labour and the poor, in particular upon toymakers. At one stage in his article he focuses upon the rocking horse maker.

'The first process is to take a pine plank and form it by jointing and glueing it, into a block (it used to be made out of solid timber, but the jointing is the better process). The block thus prepared is reduced by the drawing knife and the plane to the shape of the horse's body. It is then what we call bevelled and morticed, to make the holes into which the legs of the horse are placed. The head is shaped out of solid wood (pine), after a pattern cut out of strong pasteboard or thin plank, but we have merely the outline supplied by the pattern: what may be called the anatomy, with the eyes, the nostrils, the teeth and the several parts of the face carved out, the skill of the workman being directed altogether by his eye. The legs (of beech) are shaped without pattern, the skill of the workman again having no guide beyond his eye; and the "tenant" is then cut in the leg – the tenant being a portion of wood left on the top of the leg to be fitted in to the mortice hole made for that end of the body. Next, the head is affixed, being jointed by a great nicety of adjustment to the body of the rocking horse, and then the toy in its rough state is complete.

'After that it is what we call "worked off" – that is, each part has to be duly shaped, so that all may be in accordance: head, body, legs, without that there would be no symmetry. The "working off" is a four hours' process (taking the average sizes), and very hard work. The first layer of composition (gesso) is then applied and left to dry, which takes from eight to ten hours. The rasp is next used all over the article, and then another layer of composition is applied and then a third: this is done to get a smooth, level surface. The last application is rubbed down with glass paper.

'The horse is then painted and the legs are screwed and fitted to the "rocker", or frame, which is made before the horse is finished. It is then harnessed – we do the saddler's work ourselves; and after that the mane and tail are affixed. Then the rocking horse is complete, unless glass eyes have to be put into the head as is often the case.'

This is still basically the way that traditional rocking horses are made to this day.

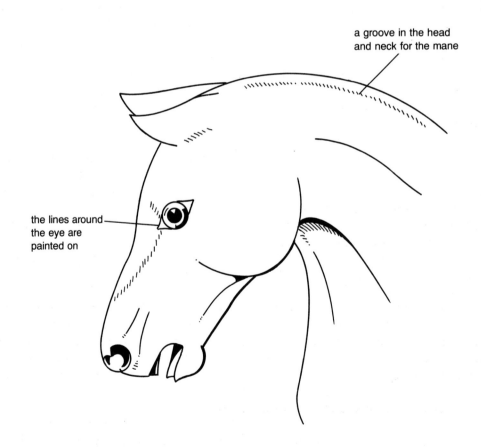

a groove in the head and neck for the mane

the lines around the eye are painted on

This type of dropped head was first used around the mid-nineteenth century.

The stance of the horse had changes too. Because it was depicting a horse going at a slower pace, the makers were able to interpret what their eyes saw better, thus the curves and legs are more natural than the stretched-out racers had been.

All the children of rich families were expected to learn to ride. Roads were so bad that by horse, or the very slow horse and carriage when the ground was firm enough, was the only way to move around the country. The big horse 52in(132cm) high with 90in(229cm) rockers was a good introduction to riding a horse, because if a real horse is seen in slow motion when it is at full gallop, it has exactly the same movements as that of these rocking horses on their boat-shaped rockers. There were plenty of nursery maids to keep an eye on too enthusiastic riders. Now it is doubtful if they would pass safety regulations as children's toys. This was the century of the great exodus of emigrants from Europe to North America, Australasia and the other colonies, and of course they took their culture with them, which meant apart from everything else rocking horses could be found worldwide. There was also the Industrial Revolution, which meant that fortunes were being made, not by just the nobility, but also a new up-and-coming middle class who could also afford large houses with large nurseries, which all *had* to have rocking horses.

To keep pace with this ever-growing demand, the making of the horses moved from the estate workshop to organized factories and still the demand grew, so they started being imported from America to Britain. The big problem with this was that those very big boat-shaped rockers were difficult to pack. Just before 1880 W. Marqua of Cincinnati, United States of America invented a new type of stand that could be packed flat for transportation and quickly assembled afterwards. This was the pillar stand, swinger stand, American stand or safety stand. This stand consisted of a wooden platform with two upright, turned pillars, with a wooden plank at the top holding the pillars in position. Two wooden parallel bars were suspended by two inverted U-shaped metal rods from the top plank and the horses hooves were fixed to the parallel bars, which could swing to and fro, moving the horse in a very similar way to a rocker, but not quite (this was a much smoother, more restricted ride). The reason it was known as the 'safety stand' was because it was almost impossible to tip over through riding too enthusiastically. Other advantages were that little fingers and toes were not squashed under rockers; they got bashed in the shins instead. There was hardly any 'travel' of the rocking horse. The old-type rockers marked wooden floors and slid along the floor at the end of each rock, great fun for the rider, but not for house-proud parents. This new stand was such a success that the boat rocker went out of fashion and gradually fewer and fewer were made.

By the turn of the twentieth century the rocking horse's popularity had grown so much that it had outstripped all other types of toy and stood supreme as king of the nursery. Manufacturers were turning them out in their thousands, the most successful being G. & J. Lines Ltd of London who produced 1,000 a year. They were only one of about a hundred factories in London alone who were making them, and there was all the rest of the world.

Much of the Lines Brothers' popularity must have been because of the quality of the carving. Even after all these years it is

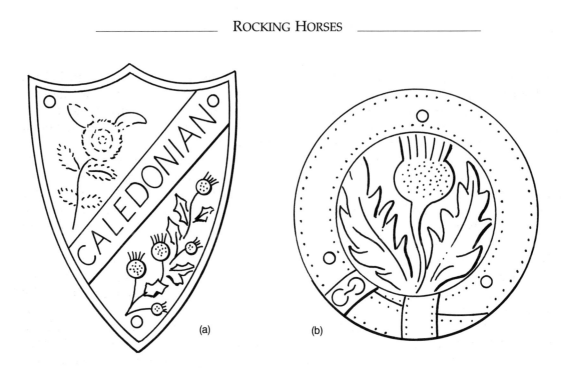

(a)   (b)

Two logos of G. & J. Lines Ltd. (a) Caledonian refers to the street where the factory was located. (b) A later version with their name stamped around the border was registered in 1910.

still a pleasure to look at the way the heads and ears were carved, made to different sizes and standards for different types of customer, but all with the same eye for detail. Obviously proud of their work, they were one of the few manufacturers who put their name on the horses they produced.

An old lady became quite misty-eyed when she was looking at one of these lovely old horses and said, 'We used to have a rocking horse like this one in the nursery when I was a child. I didn't like fatty bacon so I used to fiddle with it until nurse had finished hers and had gone down to the kitchen to get the next course, then I would take the pummel out of Dobbin (the one used for girls to ride side-saddle) and push all the fatty bacon inside. Nurse never found out and I still don't like fatty bacon.'

So restorers, watch out! Besides all the marbles, toy soldiers, pencils and other bits and pieces, that come out of the middle of an old horse you might come across dried up bits of bacon!

At the end of the nineteenth century many innovations were tried out and patents were taken out involving such things as springs and metal pieces added to the frame, but none seem to have stood the test of time. The first and most successful has been the galloper tricycle, which was a French invention. There are variations, but basically it was a prancing dapple grey, fully carved horse, with horsehair mane and tail and leather saddle, the whole thing being mounted on three, pedal-driven spoked metal wheels, steered by wooden handlebars that protruded above the horse's neck. Queen Victoria's children played on these when they were confined to the upper stories of Buckingham Palace, while suffering from whooping cough.

Rocking horses were still made during the First World War, but to a lesser extent, by the older men who didn't go to war, but it was the beginning of the decline, which became more and more marked in the 1920s and 1930s. With worldwide depression there was not so much money available for luxuries. Tarmacadam was invented, roads were levelled and covered, which meant travel became so much easier, and horses were no longer the main source of transport. In fact horses were not happy on these hard surfaces that made their hooves slip, and learning to ride to be mobile was no longer necessary.

In the 1920s there was another fashion change. Women were becoming more assertive and were allowed to take a more positive role outside the home and were also allowed to ride astride a horse, instead of side-saddle, which in turn was reflected in the rocking horses. They lost the holes to put the pummels in for the girls to learn to ride side-saddle.

New mechanical toys became the favourites. The children could still copy their parents in play because they had pedal cars and bicycles. This was the time when many a family rocking horse was left in the attic or garage to rot, given away, or even thrown out or burnt.

During the Second World War many, many more rocking horses became casualties of the fighting and the manufacture eventually stopped in Europe. The factories were taken over for the war effort, and the making of odd ones by individual people, a practice that had gone on for generations, stopped too because of the shortage of time and materials. Also there were too many other things that crowded it out.

At peace again and with restrictions lifted people developed a renewed interest in horse-riding, purely for pleasure, helped enormously by television that showed racing, showjumping, gymkhanas and enjoying the great outdoors, which included pony-trekking.

With a completely new generation of makers and the invention of new materials, it follows that there have been new ideas of how a rocking horse should be made, giving a wide choice of styles and materials used for rocking horses. The rockers have made a comeback, in a modified version, by not being so deep. Now there is a choice of stand or rockers by most makers.

Apart from the traditional painted wooden horse, there are those made from laminated plywood and clear varnished. The laminations show up sharply the contours of the horse in the colourings of the different types of wood used in the layers to make up the laminations. This type of horse is very often used as a piece of sculpture and used more to look at than ride, a trend that is growing for almost all types of rocking horses, including the old antique ones.

Another type is a moulded fibreglass horse. Very often the mould has been

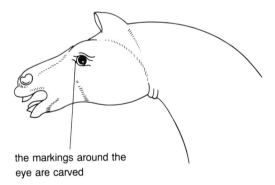

the markings around the eye are carved

Representation of the head of an antique horse from about the turn of the nineteenth century.

made from a nineteenth-century horse and needs quite close inspection to see that it is not made of wood. The giveaway is that you don't nail the harness on as you would a wooden one.

Stuffed horses have been with us for over a hundred years. They used to have about a 5in(128mm) ×4in(102mm) piece of softwood running the length of the body, to which softwood legs were nailed. The 1in(25mm) thick neck was also slotted into the same piece of wood and, a slightly carved head with no ears, but with carved nose and mouth, was slotted and nailed on to the top of the neck. The whole of the neck, body and tops of the legs were padded out with either hay or sawdust, held in a sacking cover. The whole horse, except for his nose and mouth were covered in a calf-hide with hair attached, handsewn in place. Slots were cut so that the hide ears could protrude, and almond-shaped slits for the glass eyes to show. These padded horses were either on swinger stands or modified rockers. Now the idea is very similar, but the stuffing is usually foam and the coat is fur fabric. Not so realistic but very cuddly.

Metal rocking horses were tried for a time, but went out of favour. The two main types were a metal tubular supported seat with matching rockers and a rubber moulded head with a handle at each side for a child to hold. Variations of this are still made. The other was an all-pressed metal horse with springs, so that the rider could bounce along on it. Both types were only meant for children of five years and under.

A number of people are producing rocking horses as an art form, with the horses prancing in unusual ways – this carving is a long process which is reflected in the price. One of the more traditional styles has a small animal, such as a dog or rabbit carved on to the rocker and so placed that it can be used as a step for a small child to mount. Others are making them all in hardwoods e.g. beech or mahogany and clear varnishing so that the wood grain and the different colourings show up.

So from humble beginnings, centuries ago, we have this rich and varied style of childhood playmate. One wonders if it would have developed at all if we hadn't had the patronage of kings, including our present Royal Family who have quite a few between them. Just as important, with our damp climate making travelling so difficult in the past, rocking horses provided a pleasurable way to practise riding indoors.

Though now we have this large range of styles and materials used in the making of rocking horses, the traditional painted wooden horse (usually dapple grey) mounted on its rockers or swinger stand, is still the firm favourite and it is the construction details of this type of horse that will be explained in this book.

Important Note

This book contains a number of plans for constructing different types of rocking horse (*see* pages 72–73, 81–82, 91–94, 102–104, 106–109, 118–121 and 130–133). When transcribing details, apply the enlargement factors given for each plan. To draw the plans full size, enlarge the squares (grid) to the appropriate size (i.e. ×2 or ×3, etc.). Plot in with dots the positions of the elements of the plan where they cross the grid lines. Join these dots to form the finished plan.

CHAPTER TWO

GETTING STARTED

A well-made rocking horse, provided it is treated with respect, will last for many years. Some of those still in use are nearly 200 years old. Generations of children will have something which is a playmate, rather than a plaything. They even become a family friend, so it is well worth following some basic principles in its construction to obtain a good result. Every horse can be made to look different and reflect the maker's style even when using the same pattern.

WOOD

The wood needs to be well seasoned and dry, free from dry rot, wet rot and insect infestation, such as woodworm. Until wood has actually gone rotten it is still 'live' inasmuch as it is able to absorb water and hold it, then just as easily when the atmosphere is right, expel it. The wood will swell up with water or contract when expelling water, depending on the dampness of the air around it. If, for instance, the

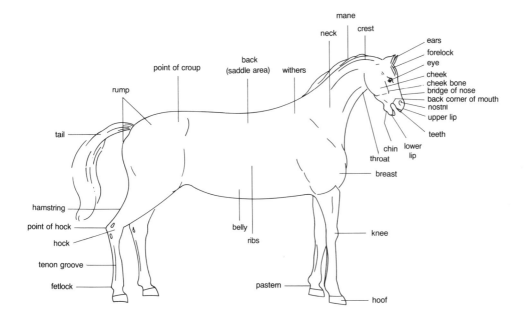

Points of the horse, as used on a rocking horse.

horse has been in a damp garden shed, two weeks spent in a centrally-heated, or air-conditioned environment will stabilize the wood before the first seal is painted on. This drying must be done slowly. A high source of heat for a few hours is more likely to dry the surface only. This causes the surface to shrink, leaving the inner wood still plimmed up with damp, which will in turn cause tension throughout, usually relieved by the wood or joins splitting open. Sealing usually stops this constant change in the water content of the wood, once it is reduced to its lowest level, as it stops further shrinking or cracking. However, if it is put near a high heat source, e.g. radiator or sun streaming through glass, or the wood is of such poor quality and so porous that it stays unstable, even with the best of sealers cracking may still occur. No sealers are perfect, but most will work unless conditions are extreme.

Nearly all rocking horses made in Britain from about 1800 to 1940 were made with a pine body and head, with beech legs and rockers, or hoof rails and pillars of the swinger stand, the other planks being pine. This combination is very good as the countless rocking horses of this period that are still being used bear witness.

Some other woods that can be used are sycamore or lime for body and head with beech legs. Sycamore, and especially lime, which is very stable, are very good and easy to carve where the wood is chunky, but not very strong in long lengths, such as the hoof rails, that children often stand on when mounting a horse, as part of a swinger stand. It is definitely not strong enough for rockers as it is subject to breaking across the grain, known as cross breaks. Ash is strong and makes good rockers. Oak and elm are both heavy woods and although strong, would make

a horse cumbersome to move if all the horse and stand were of the same wood. This also applies to mahogany, although it does give a good deep colour when polished. Mahogany is found wild in the tropical rain forests, as are other suitable tropical woods, such as jelutong and iroko. These are therefore undesirable for use in modern times, because of conservation, but they are beginning to be plantation grown and it is worth seeking out timber merchants who can supply these plantation-grown woods if it is imperative to have a tropical wood.

Although the beech and pine horse is the normal construction, there is at least one maker who makes the legs, pillars and hoof rail of pine also, and these have stood the test of some thirty years or more.

The legs and hoof rails are one-and-a-half times as thick as the normal size and the pillars of the stand are very thick and square at the base, tapering slightly towards the top. Many of these rocking horses are only just beginning to show their age.

The woods mentioned so far are available in the British Isles, but many countries have locally grown types of wood that can be used. The criteria are that the wood should be dry, have a low water content and give as little movement as possible, which means it must not be prone to warping and splitting easily and should be workable. For the body American white pine is an example of unsuitable wood as it is unstable, but American yellow pine is excellent; it carves reasonably well, is not too heavy and once glued together doesn't warp and move under normal conditions.

The legs, rockers or pillars and hoof rails must be of a good strong wood that is not subject to cross breaks. The rest of the wood for the stand or spacers for the rockers can be a slightly lighter weight of wood. A rule of thumb is that a close fine grain will usually be much better than an open coarse absorbent grain. If you are not sure, the best way is to seek out and ask a local expert. Second-hand wood is another source. Wood from demolition can be dry and well seasoned, and providing it has no rot or worm holes, it can be especially good for the head and body. A good buy sometimes, is a grimy piece of beam, providing you are aware of the big snags, like removing old nails, and can identify it, just the thing that a lovely rocking horse can be made from and not just a junk piece with a load of flaws in it. Air drying, or seasoning, takes roughly one year for each 1in(25mm) thickness of wood, depending also on the density of the wood. A much quicker way is to have wood kiln dried, which will take out the water content in a matter of hours; in the case of lime wood down to 8 per cent water content. A very good way of making wood usable quickly, but it is no good for very thick dense wood. Also, it should be remembered that although the water content has been reduced to single figures, the wood is still able to and will reabsorb water if the conditions are right to do so.

TIPS ON CONSTRUCTION

The carving of a rocking horse can be completely to your own design, but there are a few points of stress where good joinery is needed if it is to be ridden and not just ornamental. The join at the top of the leg where hardwood legs meet softwood body is under stress the whole time the horse is in use so this really must be a good fit. The hoof where it meets the rocker/hoof rail needs to be cut carefully

and bolted securely. If the bolt hole is made at a slightly downward angle from the outside of the hoof, through the hoof and through the rocker/hoof rail, the bolt is not so likely to bend with age if there becomes any mismatch through wood shrinkage or the bolt becoming loose.

Hooves are bolted to the rocker or swinger bars so that they can be taken apart for storage, transport or for repairs, and nothing else has been found that makes a better job of these particular needs.

Another important factor is to get the centre of gravity as low as is practical without spoiling the fun of the ride so that even with hard use the rocking horse will not fall over. The legs should slant out sideways $12\frac{1}{2}°$ (12.5°) from upright giving stability without being too obviously splayed.

With a large horse (30in(762mm) or more in body length) on bow rockers, the legs need to be at full stretch and the rockers long enough so that at the end of the rock the horse and rider are still in line as they would be if it was a real horse just landing after jumping a fence and not as in the diagram overleaf where horse and rider would end up on their noses. With any horse on rockers the weight and balance of the horse can be partly evened up by using a thick block of wood at the rump end of the hollow oblong middle section of the body, which counteracts the extra weight of the horse's head. The rider will do the rest as he sits slightly back from the central point of the horse.

Rockers should not be cut as a half of a circle, but more like two-thirds (66 per cent) of the long side of an oval with the centre of each of the rockers where they rest on the ground being flattened off for about 6in(152mm) so that when the rider

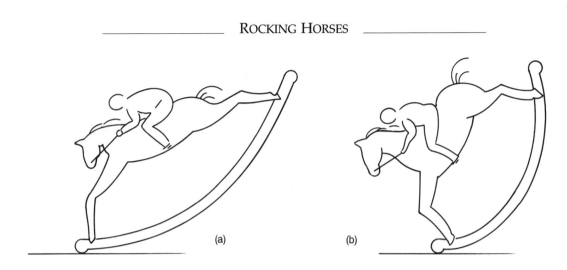

Designing a horse on bow rockers. (a) Correct. (b) Incorrect.

is mounting the horse will not start to rock immediately. In fact a little push on the part of the rider when seated should be needed to start the movement. On the stand the main points of stress are at the top and bottom of the pillars, therefore to give the best fixings possible the stubs of the pillars need to go right through the top rail and both bottom planks. Another point to note is where the swinger bar is clamped to the top plank, since this clamp has to give full movement to the swinger bar without having any slack, which would cause clonking, wear, and be unnerving for a timid rider.

The positioning of the swinger bars themselves can give different effects. When the horse is at rest, if the swinger bars are in a vertical position with the clamps holding the bars onto the top rail being straight above the point where the swinger bars go through the hoof rail for fixing, the horse will give a perfectly horizontal ride with no bucking or rearing, which takes some of the fun out of it. The correct position for the clamp is about 2in(51mm) towards the end of the top plank from where each of the pillar stubs come through the top rail. It should then go through the hoof rail at an angle of about 25° from the vertical

towards the centre of this rail. This will make the front and rear of the horse lift alternately as it is ridden, giving a more realistic feeling of a horse going at speed. If the angle of the swingers is too great, it will bring the horse high up from its stand, which looks ungainly and alters the centre of gravity making the rocking horse unstable. A clearance of 3in(76mm) to 4in(102mm) between the stand's top rail and the belly of the horse is enough.

Screw or Dowel

It is much quicker to use nails or screws and glue to hold the different parts of the horse together, but for long-lasting results it is much better to use wooden dowels. Most nails and screws are subject to rust and a rusty nail or screw expands and will gradually either loosen a joint or split the wood before it rusts right through. Rust also causes dark stains which gradually rot the wood. The other problem of using nails or even rustless screws is that metal expands and contracts with heat or cold at different rates to wood, so the fixings slowly become loose. Screws are excellent for holding a glued joint together while it is drying, providing they are removed and replaced by wooden dowels when they have done their job.

There are places where screws and nails are better than dowels. Nails are best for attaching a mane of the type made out of a horse or cow's tail and cured with the hair still attached to the leather. Manes are the first thing to wear out; having it nailed in place makes it easy to lift off what remains of the mane, nails and all, fill in the nail holes and nail on a replacement mane. Screws are used in the ends of rockers to hold the spacer bars in place, because children often stand on the bars to get a different type of ride when the seat of the horse is occupied. Dowels are apt to cross break, and screws are found to be much stronger in withstanding the weight.

Leather

When leather and not plastic is used for the tack on a horse it is cowhide of different thicknesses from $\frac{1}{16}$in(1.5mm) to $\frac{1}{8}$in (3mm) thick, taken from different parts of the hide, giving either suppleness for the saddle or the strength needed for such items as the stirrup-straps and reins. Sheepskin is occasionally used on the saddle. These two types of hide are used almost universally as they are readily available and reasonably priced.

Glue

Traditionally the old horses were glued together with animal glue. This had to be kept warm in a container over a pan of hot water, because it would solidify if cooled. Keeping the glue pot was the job of the youngest apprentice. The animal glue was fine when there was nothing better, but its drawback was that it was water soluble.

More than one person has gone to retrieve the family rocking horse from the back of the garage after many years of storage only to find when it was picked up that it fell to pieces, the glue having absorbed too much moisture from the damp atmosphere and dissolved away. Two modern families of glues, epoxy resin and latex make a much more permanent seal than the old glues, providing the right type is used. Epoxy resin glue has very good bonding for wood and yet it has just enough 'give' to allow for that very small amount of movement that there is in all wood, without cracking the joints open. Indeed it has been found that the glue is often stronger than the wood when an attempt has been made to take apart a join. Latex glue stays slightly malleable even when dry and is excellent for use with leather and hair, which is not static.

HOW TO MEASURE A ROCKING HORSE

The correct way to measure the size of a rocking horse is from breast to rump, leaving out the curves – in other words the length of its body. All other measurements can vary a great deal depending on how big a stride the horse has and the position of the head or the maker's designs. There are usually three categories of sizes: 23in(584mm) and under for the small size, suitable for children up to about five years old, 24in(610mm) to 28in(711mm) body is the most popular medium size as it will take a child of up to about ten to twelve years old and the large 29in(737mm) or over size, which will take the weight of a small adult. As you can see the larger ones can last a boy or girl all through childhood, which very few other toys can.

WORKING CONDITIONS

Good lighting is essential and safer, for good workmanship. Fluorescent light is the best substitute, but there is nothing to beat daylight when seeking out any small flaws prior to the last sanding being done. As there is a great deal of sanding to be done and the sawdust that comes off is very fine and covers everything, either sand in the open air where the sawdust will disperse, or have a dust extractor unit which can be attached to all the machinery that creates sawdust. The sawdust from the wood can cause irritation and infection of the nose and bronchial tubes, so always use a proper dust mask for any dusty work, or spraying. It doesn't have to be an expensive complicated mask; the simple ones remove the dust particles quite well from the air you actually breathe. Ear protectors are also a must when using noisy machinery. A dry warm, but not hot, workshop is not only for the benefit of the worker, it also keeps all the wood in the correct condition.

REGULATIONS

Many countries, including all the countries of the European Economic Community, have strict laws governing children's toys, which regulate what they are made from and how they are made. Always check that all paints are suitable for toys and that other parts, such as leather and hair, are cured to high standards and contain no lead, chromium or traces of other excluded chemicals above the allowed amount. Rocking horses that are offered for sale might be required to be prominently labelled with the maker's name and address, also clearly stating what sort of accidents could occur when the rocking horse is in use if not fully supervised, such as the trapping of small fingers and toes.

TIME

In 1851 Mayhew stated that about 1,500 rocking horses (of all different sizes) were made each year by thirty men. This equals roughly one per week by one man and probably represents sixty to seventy hours of hard work.

The time taken today very much depends on the skill of the maker and how the horse is made. Slapping a horse together and nailing it and coating it with gesso to cover the faults could possibly halve the time that a carefully constructed, well- finished horse would take. Assuming the latter and that it is the first horse the maker has made with a well-equipped do-it-yourself workshop, a rough estimate is that the actual construction will be in excess of eight hours for the plywood doll-sized horse, ten hours for the flat horses, forty hours for the small horses, fifty hours for the medium sizes and sixty hours for the large horses. This is assuming that the maker is familiar with all his tools both for wood and leather.

Swinger Stand

If a rocking horse on a swinger stand is placed in such a position that it is always mounted from the same side, so that the rider uses the hoof rail to mount each time, the swinger bars can go out of true in time, especially if it is a large horse. The horse gets a lean, causing extra wear on the moving parts. The suggestion is that the horse is turned the other way periodically so as to even up the wear.

CHAPTER THREE

TOOLS

Nearly all the tools that are an absolute necessity when making a rocking horse are the same common everyday tools which are found in a handyman's collection. Of course if you have, in addition, electric powered tools, it will cut down the time in the making, lessening the manpower used and making it easier to be accurate. The one exception is the use of a band-saw; without this to cut out the shapes of head, legs and rockers (if using these) the making of a rocking horse would get very tedious. The cutting out of the shapes should take under an hour to do, so it is worth considering hiring time on someone else's band-saw if you do not have your own. An electric jigsaw can be used, but it is slow and can be expensive as the blade will heat up quickly, blunting it and causing burn marks on the wood if you use a hardwood such as beech. The other option is a fretsaw and plenty of manpower and time.

Below are lists of tools and their specific uses with regard to the making and restoring of rocking horses. The first list has those tools that really are a must for all but the toddler's and doll's horse, the second are tools that make work easier, the third are some electrical tools that are a help, but not absolutely necessary and the fourth are a few tools that are used only for restoration and making accessories.

There is a short list at the beginning of the instructions on how to make each of the horses, of which tools will be needed for that particular horse, for instance the toddler's horse needs very few tools but restoring a horse uses many more.

LIST ONE

Pencil A carpenter's pencil is excellent for straight lines, but an ordinary soft pencil is sometimes better for sharp curves.

Rules A steel rule that can also double up as a reliable straight edge is useful for stands, horses and restorations. A tape rule is needed as well all through the new work and restoration.

G Clamps A selection of clamps 2in (51mm) up to 6in(152mm) are useful for restorations. The minimum of four of 4in(102mm) to 6in(152mm) size are needed in the making of new horses.

Electric Hand Drill Like the band-saw, making a rocking horse or restoring one without one of these would become very labour intensive. It is used throughout the making and restoring of the horses and stands and needs to be compatible with the drill stand and not too large. Alternatively, use a large drill for the stand and a small one for work where mobility is important, such as sanding.

Drill Stand This is used in conjunction with an electric hand drill, and is used in quite a few operations where a vertical hole is needed. Its size depends on the size of the hand drill.

Band-saw This needs a ¼in(6mm) four or six skip blade when cutting out the head, legs and rockers (if used) of a new horse and similar parts on a restoration. If it is used instead of a circular saw for cutting wood in straight lengths to required sizes, a very wide blade should be used. A band-saw with a 12in(305mm) throat is needed. Saws with smaller throats can be used, but it is difficult to cut out the heads of the larger horses with these.

Drills Different sizes of both twist and spade drills are used with both hand and pillar drills.

Countersink Bit To countersink all screw holes so that all screws are below the surface for safety.

Vice A wood vice is best, provided it will hold at least a 3in(76mm) thick piece of wood. Other means of holding the work still can be used; the criteria is that the tool must be able to hold the wood steady enough to carve and or drill without marking it.

Saws A cross-cut saw can be used for cutting straight lengths of wood if no other saw is available; it is also used to cut out the leg sockets on the new horses. A tenon-saw has many uses for new work and restoration. A tenon-saw with fine teeth is an extra bonus when sawing out the lips to make the teeth.

Screwdrivers One large screwdriver with a flat blade, thin enough to slot into a No. 8 screw (the blade may need filing down to do this), and one medium screwdriver, also able to slot into No. 8 screws. Alternatively screwdrivers that can slot into pozi drive or Phillip's screws. The uses are many all through both the making and restoring of horses and their stands.

Chisels Straight chisels with bevelled edges. One 1in(25mm) to 1½in(38mm) depending on the individual's choice, used for general carving of the horse. A disadvantage of this type of chisel initially is that with softwood, such as pine, it can split the wood easily, but this can be used to advantage with practice. One ⅜in(9mm) straight chisel of the same type as the former. Used in confined areas on the horses.

Gouges Canal straight form gouge, one 1in(25mm) to 1½in(38mm) depending on the individual's own choice and used for general carving of the horse; it doesn't split softwood, but a straight chisel is still needed to make creases such as around the jaw. One ½in(13mm) canal straight form gouge to carve ears and nostrils and fine detail of muscles, etc.

Mallet Wooden, round or square; it is just a matter of choice. Weight is more important; too light and more force is required, too heavy and more effort is used than is needed. No chisel or gouge should be tapped with anything but a wooden mallet.

Spokeshave or Draw Knife Used for general carving instead of a chisel on both the new horses and restorations, especially the legs, but not a must if surforms are used.

Paint Brushes A number of these may be needed and a different brush should be used for each different colour or varnish. Even with the most careful cleaning, smudges of the former colour are likely to come through the hairs to spoil the work. A 1½in(38mm) size is suitable for most jobs, small ones for painting the mouth and teeth and very thin ones for small markings such as around the eyes.

Oil Stones Both flat and slip are needed for sharpening chisels, plane blades and gouges.

Surform One round and one half-round, useful in shaping the nose, ears, chin and between the legs. These are very good at controlling how much wood is being removed.

Planes A smoothing plane is useful for general flattening of surfaces ready for gluing etc, while a jack plane is suitable for smoothing large surfaces and especially the centre box section of the horse's body. Neither of these tools are necessary if an electric planer or planer-thicknesser is available.

Combination Square This is used to get a 90° angle when preparing wood, and for squaring of bow rockers and checking that surfaces are flat, especially when restoring. An added bonus is if a spirit level is included, which excludes the need for a separate one.

Rubber Backing Disc Attachment This is for use with an electric hand drill 5in(127mm) in diameter for holding an assortment of sanding discs, both metal cintride and ordinary abrasive discs for general sanding of horses and where appropriate the stands as well. It is very good for removing gesso on restorations. A smaller soft-backed disc can be used for awkward corners.

Sanding Discs The normal glass paper discs can be used, but ones such as garnet and aluminium oxide last much longer, removing the annoyance of having to keep stopping to change the disc. Coarse and medium are both needed for new horses and for restorations fine also. Metal cintride coarse discs are used for the first sanding away of the rough wood after carving on the horse. Cintride discs must be used with extreme care on restorations as the surface wood is old and more fragile than new wood.

Dust Mask This should be used for all dusty operations such as sanding and removing gesso. The dust from both wood and gesso can be a danger to health, causing chest infections. Thankfully the fashion not to wear a mask or ear protectors is no longer considered macho, just foolhardy. The mask does not have to be elaborate; lightweight disposable ones are sufficient.

Ear Protectors These are used when using electrical tools. Hearing fades quickly enough without helping it along!

Sandpaper As with sanding discs, garnet paper is the better, used for small patches of hand sanding where nothing else will go on new and restoration horses. Use coarse grit 60 followed by medium grit 80 and finer grits for sanding between sealers, undercoats and varnishes. Coarse grit 60 is needed for all over sanding if electric sanders (such as the orbital sander) are not being used.

Protractor This is used to mark the angles needed to be cut so that legs are in the correct positions.

Hammer This is needed for nailing on tack or nailing leather to make the removable saddle.

LIST TWO

Hand-Held Electric Planer This takes some of the hard work out of planing. It needs practice to be used properly as it has a habit of taking a large chunk out of the end of the piece of wood being planed. It is not advisable to use it on the old wood of restorations as the cut can be quite fierce.

Sash Clamps Four adjustable sash clamps or their equivalent, minimum of 12in (305mm) long. These are not imperative if there are other means, but they are the easiest way of clamping large sections of wood when glued, such as bodies. They are used for the same purposes in restorations.

Orbital Sander This is very useful for the final sanding of new or restored horses, and reduces by a great deal the time and effort needed to sand. Any grit of sanding paper can be used, depending on requirements.

Dust Extractor A necessity only if all the sanding is done in a confined space, but is also useful if it is combined with other tools such as the band-saw and electric planer-thicknesser.

Planer or Planer-Thicknesser This needs to be big enough to take at least a 10in(254mm) wide wood for the most versatile results. Smaller ones curtail their usefulness and the size of the rocking horse that can be satisfactorily planed. It is ideal for the preparation of the wood. Although not used to the same extent for restorations of the actual horses, it is good for renewing parts of swinger stands and rockers.

Wood Turning Lathe This is only used for turning pillars, and possibly spacer bars for rockers. Should be large enough to take 24in(610mm) between centres and with a throw of at least 4in(102mm) if the pillars are to be made for a large horse.

Chisels for Lathe The minimum requirements are a ¾in(19mm) deep gouge and an assortment of scraper profiles depending on what profile you want the pillars to have. If spacer bars for the dolls' horse are needed, smaller gouge and scrapers are needed.

Pillar Drill This is used instead of a hand drill and drill stand for making vertical holes. It is more accurate than a hand drill, especially for making the holes for the pillar stubs in the swinger stand base.

Electric Jigsaw Very good for cutting up large pieces of plywood this is not good for accurate small turns.

Rifler Files These are handy for all sorts of filing where it is awkward to get other tools and are good for removing gesso from odd corners on restorations. One flat and one curved round shape would do, but they are so versatile that almost any shape or size would be of use.

Spirit Level This is used for only one purpose and that is to check that the new or restored horses are sitting evenly on their rockers or swinger stand. It is not needed if there is a spirit level in the combination square.

Calipers Internal and external calipers can be used to check sizes on new horses, but are used more on restorations to be sure that new parts such as legs are exactly the same as those they are replacing.

Circular Saw This is used for the cutting of timber into the sizes required for both the horses and their stands and is used for this purpose in restorations. The blade needs to be large enough to take a minimum cut of 3in(76mm).

LIST THREE

Airbrush Attached to a compressor, this is used for spraying paint. It can be used for general painting, but with a fine nozzle is ideal for painting the dappling on dappled horses. There is good control of the amount of spray used and it can give a very realistic effect with very little practice.

Power File Used to sand in awkward places such as under the chin and between the ears. It will easily take too much wood away, especially on restorations, but with practice and a gentle touch it can be used for small pieces of carving, for example on the face and neck or on the doll-sized horse.

Electric Combination Machine There would be no need to use all the processes it is capable of doing, but it could take the place of a planer-thicknesser.

LIST FOUR

Hacksaw This is used for sawing through bolts and sometimes nails and screws that are so rusty they cannot be moved in any other way and possibly for sawing a straight line under the chin.

Strap Wrench This loosens or tightens swinger stand pillars when they have a wooden screw thread on the bottom stub.

Ball Peen Hammer Only needed for one specific job when the ends of the swinger bars that protrude out of the hoof rails need peening over. By making the ends larger, you prevent the washers coming off.

Drum Sanding This attachment for an electric hand drill has a foam drum with a circular sanding belt around its middle. It is ideal for sanding the wood of restored rocking horses as it gets it smooth, but it is so gentle that no more than the absolute minimum of wood is removed.

Rivet Punch This is used to make one type of removable bridle.

Leather Punch Used in conjunction with the rivet punch for making the holes for the rivets, it is also used for making holes in the strapping to connect with the buck-les for stirrup-straps and removable bridles.

Awl This is used for piercing leather if the harness is sewn together.

Needle Large and blunt-ended for sewing leather together, two are needed if the correct method of sewing leather together is used.

Scissors Used mostly in the making of the saddle cloth or numnah, they are also used if leatherette or plastic are used for the saddle and harness.

Knife For cutting leather.

Stitch Wheel Run over the leather where it is to be stitched, it gives an even marking of the length of the stitches.

Beeswax The thread pulled over a block of beeswax becomes coated, making it easier to use and preserves the thread.

Chisel Peen Hammer This is mainly used to nail in brass domed nails when putting on the harness.

Morticer This is only used if a traditional mortice and tenon joint is to be made. Other methods for new horses are described.

The lists could go on almost indefinitely, especially number three, but fine rocking horses and good restorations can be achieved with what has been mentioned. If the making is just a 'one-off' project then the first list will keep the cost down to the minimum, but the short lists in the front of the chapters on more specific projects should be referred to before buying any extra equipment.

CHAPTER FOUR

ACCESSORIES

TOOLS

Hammer for nailed-on saddle and bridle. Rivet punch (only used if you have removable tack; the reins are rivetted together). Leather punch for rivets, removable bridle and stirrup-straps. Knife for cutting leather. Awl for piercing the stitch marks. Stitch wheel for marking the stitch marks. Needle for stitching leather together (or two needles if using the correct leather stitching methods – these must be the correct, strong leather needles with blunted ends). Beeswax for thread lubrication. Edging tool to score an even line around the edge for stitching and neatness (optional). Chisel peen hammer for nailing brass domed nails.

MATERIALS

As materials differ depending on which you are making, a list of what is needed appears under each item. Amounts of materials required depend a great deal on the size of the horse, therefore to avoid confusion, amounts quoted are for a 26in (660mm) medium-sized horse.

SADDLES

There are many designs of saddle from a simple piece of leather or leather cloth shaped like a saddle and nailed on to the back of the horse, to very elaborate affairs that are exact replicas of racing saddles, western (cowboy) saddle and Mexican or Arab saddles. Here are four of the more usual types used, of which two have details for making.

Simple Saddle

Materials: A 15in(381mm) by 24in(610mm) piece of leather which is a minimum of $\frac{1}{16}$in(2mm) thick, or alternatively a piece of leather cloth. Two 1in(25mm) solid 'D' rings, padding to fit, 30 nails preferably brass domed, six 1in(25mm) nails, 2 yards(2 metres) of thread.

The simplest saddle is a piece of leather or leather cloth which has the centre part (seat) pear shaped, like a real saddle and has, at each side, one large rounded flap and one small rounded flap. The seat can be padded or left flat; if it is padded the padding needs enclosing securely so that it doesn't push out from under the saddle when in use. Cut the two pieces of the saddle out and also one 1in(25mm) wide 7in(178mm) long strap piece from the surplus leather/leather cloth.

For the saddle without padding lay the large piece of saddle across the horse in position. Thread a 'D' ring on either end of the long strip and double the end back under for 2in(51mm). Lay this also across the horse and 2in(51mm) from the neck end of the saddle nail with three nails each side, through the double thickness of the strip and the large piece of saddle just below the edge of where the top piece will be nailed at the edges of the seat area. Put the top, smaller piece of leather/leather cloth across the horse so that the small flaps cover the 'D' rings and nail around the edges of the seat area.

With the padded version the strip with the 'D' rings is laid across the large piece of saddle and the ends looped back above the line of the edge of the seat and held there. The top smaller saddle piece is laid on top and the two sewn together around the seat area leaving enough room to push in the padding, before completing the sewing, and nailing on around the stitch line.

If made in leather which can be treated occasionally with leather soap, this saddle is very durable and easy to use for children of all ages.

Traditional Saddle

Materials: A 15in(381mm) by 24in(610mm) piece of leather which is a minimum of $\frac{1}{16}$(2mm) thick. One strip of leather $\frac{3}{4}$in(19mm) to 1in(25mm) wide and the length of the wooden backrest. Padding to fit. Thirty to forty domed nails. A 9in(229mm) by 9in(229mm) approximately, piece of cloth, such as plain cotton to hold the padding in position. Approx. 2 yards(2 metres) of thread.

A copy from the nineteenth-century rocking horse is a leather saddle using a wooden backrest which keeps the saddle seat sloping forwards, towards the neck of

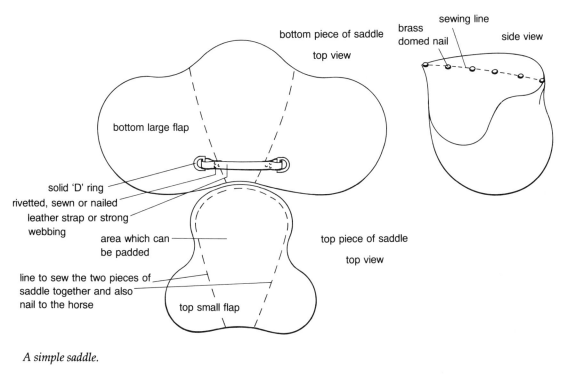

bottom piece of saddle

top view

brass domed nail

sewing line

side view

bottom large flap

solid 'D' ring rivetted, sewn or nailed leather strap or strong webbing

area which can be padded

top piece of saddle

top view

line to sew the two pieces of saddle together and also nail to the horse

top small flap

A simple saddle.

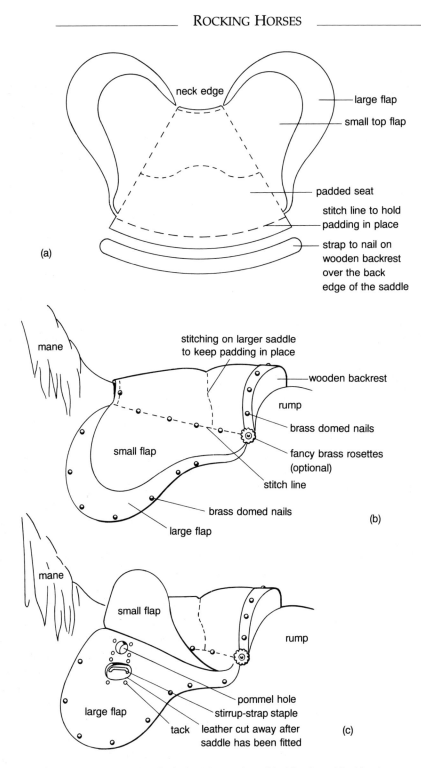

The traditional saddle with a wooden backrest (a) top view; (b) side view; (c) side view with small top flap lifted.

the horse. The wooden backrest is fixed into the horse; further details of this are in the chapter on restoration. The leather seat is triangular in shape with the point cut off at the neck end and is padded. It has one large and one small flap each side. Cut all the pieces out, four flaps, one seat and leather strip. The smaller flap is sewn to the side of the leather seat in the same seam used to sew on the cloth backing of the seat that holds the padding in place. The seat and two flaps are now put on the horse and temporarily held in place with two nails, one at the front and one at the back. The large flap is now pushed under the seat just far enough so that when the saddle is nailed on the small flap side of the stitching line, the nails also go through the top of the large flap and into the horse. Do the same on the other side, forming a row of brass headed nails in two lines down the sides of the saddle. Check that the strip of leather is the length and width of the wooden backrest. The back edge of the seat should be resting on the top of the wooden backrest; nail the strip of leather over the top of this to neaten the saddle and hold the seat in place. This strip of leather gives a nice finish to the saddle and also gives the maker a chance to make a pattern of the brass domed nails used. There are no girth straps fitted to this or the previous saddle. For durability and ease of use there is nothing between this and the saddle before.

Carved Saddle

Materials: 1/16in(2mm) thick soft leather, latex glue.

Some modern rocking horse designs include a saddle that is carved in wood and screwed on to the back of the horse, being just a carved seat, tipped up at the back, dipping down in the middle and rising to a small pummel at the front and no flaps. It can look very good on an unpainted horse, but there are problems when it comes to covering them with leather. The best way is before the seat is screwed into position, cut out a paper pattern first, to check that everything will fit. Cut out the leather and check it against the saddle again, screw the seat into position and following the instructions on the glue container, glue the leather straight onto the wood of the moulded seat, smoothing it into place. If the leather is soft and pliable it should mould to the shape of the saddle.

Removable Saddle

The saddle which is much more fun, but harder to make and a little more complicated for the rider to use, is the removable saddle. This type of saddle looks more like the real thing with a rounded tipped up back, a small pummel at the front and is stiffened with a wooden former through the middle. Covered in leather it can be used as the start for teaching a small child how to look after tack and open up a whole new range of games to play with the rocking horse.

In the making of this type of saddle the most important thing is to make sure that the saddle cannot slip when the rider puts their foot in the stirrup to mount. One good way of doing this is to carve the backbone ridge down the back of the horse from croup to the base of the neck (withers) and carve the underside of the saddle former to match; the underside is then covered with suede leather. When the girth strap of this saddle is tight there is no way that the saddle can slip over the ridge. It does rely though on the rider checking the girth, before mounting, which many children forget to do.

A more positive method that does not need a backbone ridge is to have two wooden pegs (½in(13mm) diameter will do) fitted into the underside of the wooden former and these correspond with two holes drilled into the horse's back. This way even if the girth strap is not tight, the saddle will still not slip round. Again the underside of the saddle former is padded with either suede leather or sheepskin to protect the paint on the horse.

STIRRUP-STRAPS

Materials: One ⅛in(3mm) thick by ½in(13mm) to ¾in(19mm) wide straps, 48in(1,220mm) long. Two buckles to match the width of the strapping, two rivets for each or sewing thread, two custom-made U staples.

The common methods of fixing the stirrups are firstly, to gouge out an area 1in(25mm) high, 1½in(38mm) along the body and ⁵⁄₁₆in(16mm) deep, at each side and 1in(25mm) lower than the straight line of the edge of the saddle seat, but far enough forward so that it will be covered by the small saddle flap. Along this depression a U-shaped staple is hammered in, leaving a gap of ⁵⁄₁₆in(16mm) behind it, over the large saddle flap, but under the small flap. The staples are made of ⅛in(3mm) heavy-duty stiff wire ¾in (19mm) at the bottom of the U with two 1¼in(32mm) long prongs (*see* right). Cut the 48in(1,220mm) strap in half, sew or rivet a buckle at one end of each piece and punch a line of holes at the other end and first put this end through the

stirrup and then loop round the U staple to make an adjustable stirrup-strap. The depressions in the side of the horse help to keep the stirrup-straps neatly against the horses sides. With removable saddles and some nailed-on simple-type saddles, metal 'D' rings from which the adjustable stirrup-straps can be hung, are on straps and are incorporated into the saddle.

The second way is to sew or rivet the stirrups on to the ends of the long strip of the same type of sturdy leather as the adjustable straps. Hang the strip over the horse's back, close to the base of the neck, making sure the stirrups are of an even height, and either screw or nail the strip in position. This is done before the saddle is put on. The disadvantage of this type of stirrup-strap is that the large flap of the saddle is usually nailed over the top of part of it and with time gets torn or the nails

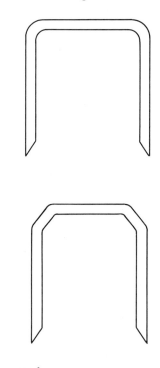

Stirrup-strap staples.

come out. There is no adjustment either for altering the strap as children grow, but it is easy to make and attach.

CRUPPER

Materials: One piece of strapping 9in(228mm) to 15in(381mm) long, depending on how big a loop is used, and four to ten brass domed nails.

A crupper on a rocking horse has no useful function. On a real horse it is used to stop the saddle sliding forward when the horse lands from a jump. The crupper is therefore only decoration and reaches from the back of the saddle seat or wooden backrest, around the tail and is looped back on itself, nailed in place with domed brass nails. On a removable saddle, in most cases it is more bother for a child to use, than it is worth and therefore is rarely present.

MARTINGALE

Materials: ½in(13mm) to ¾in(19mm) strap approximately 40in(1,016mm) long. Ten brass domed nails, or for a removable one, three to four rivets and one ¾in(19mm) or 1in(25mm) 'D' ring and one buckle the same width as the strapping.

The martingale is likewise only decoration on a rocking horse. On a real horse it is to stop the saddle sliding backwards when the horse takes off for a jump. The decorative rocking horse martingale is looped around the base of the neck ending in a V in the middle of the breast; from the V onward a piece of strapping goes down between the horses legs and is fastened off

with a nail at some convenient place out of sight. The centre of the V is a favourite place to put a brass or ribbon rosette. Dome or fancy headed brass nails and brass rosettes put in a pattern along this strapping can make the martingale look very attractive. A similar martingale can be made to be removable. The ends of the V and the end of the strap going between the legs are sewn or rivetted round a 'D' ring and the other end of the strap going under the belly, having a loop (which is sewn, rivetted or a buckle put on for adjustment) for the girth strap to go through.

NUMNAH

Materials: 18in(457mm) by 12in(305mm) piece of cloth and 60in(1,524mm) decorative border, sewing cotton, twenty brass domed nails.

Numnah or saddle cloth is an under blanket and is used on a real horse to stop the saddle chafing and soak up sweat which with the chafing can cause saddle sores. Again on a rocking horse it is only decoration, but it does give a chance to add some colour to the horse. The numnah fits across the top of the back of the horse under the saddle, between the withers and croup and extends down either side of the body to below the large flap of the saddle, the lower corners being rounded at the front and making an extended point towards the rear of the horse. Any durable material can be used for this, the favourite being upholstery weight, plain coloured velvet, with a decorative trim. This is not very practical to use with the two types of removable saddles, as the numnah tends to slide around too much for children to cope with.

GIRTH

> Materials: 15in(381mm) approximately of strapping for a nailed-on saddle and 30in(762mm) for a removable saddle and buckle to match the width of the strap, two rivets or thread.

The girth is a wide webbing or elasticated strap which holds the saddle in position on a real horse. If it is fitted on a rocking horse with nailed-on saddle it must be positioned slightly forward of centre of the belly and each end tacked up out of sight under the large flap of the saddle. However as this is only decorative and very little can be seen below the flaps, it is very rarely fitted. With a removable saddle it can be very important in keeping the saddle in position with the version that has no pegs. It should be either a strong wide leather strap or a webbing type with a buckle to match, rivetted or sewn in a position where it is under the large flap and will not chafe the rider's legs. The girth strap has a second use in that it can teach a child why a girth strap is needed and how to buckle it up.

BRIDLES

Materials vary and are shown with each type of bridle. There are three main versions of bridles, two that are nailed on and one that is removable. The exact location and number of straps used for a bridle varies in different countries as there are a great variety of styles of bridles, some by custom and some for a specific use. The three versions here are of the common British style, but they can be adapted to make many other styles.

Nailed-on Bridle

> Materials: 40in(1,016mm) long ½in(13mm) wide strapping, sixteen ½in(13mm) brass domed nails.

This is the most popular nailed-on version used with a bit (*see* right). Nail a piece of strapping above the back corner of the mouth and going over the bridge of the nose right round behind the chin and under the jaw and back again, butting the two ends together. This is the nose band. Loop an end of the strapping through the ring of the bit and bend it back on itself, nailing it above the back corner of the mouth. Extend the strapping up the cheek, over the head, behind the ears, down the other cheek and loop through the other bit ring. Cut off surplus, bend back on itself and nail just above the back corner of the mouth. Put nails in half-way up the cheeks and at the temples. This is the head strap. For the brow band, stretch a length of strap the right size under the forelock and just below the ears, from one temple to the other, butting and nailing the ends where they meet the long head strap and the brass domed nail holding it. At this same point butt and nail another strap to go from the temple, under the throat and up to the other temple to complete the bridle. You can use more brass domed nails. Brass or pretty ribbon rosettes can be nailed at the point where the three straps meet.

Closed Mouth Bridle

> Materials: ½in(13mm) wide 40in(1,016mm) long strapping, sixteen brass domed nails, two screw eyelets.

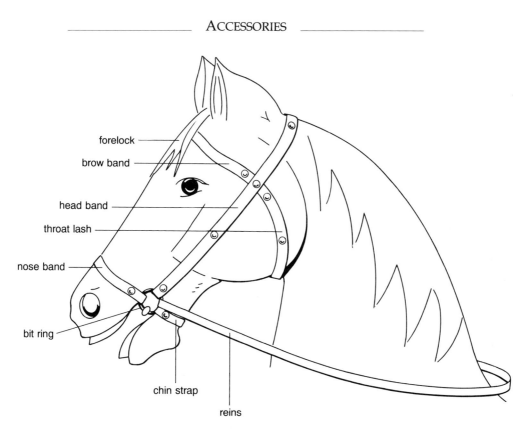

forelock

brow band

head band

throat lash

nose band

bit ring

chin strap

reins

A traditional nailed-on bridle.

A simpler version of the nailed-on bridle can be used for a horse with a closed mouth. The instructions as for the nailed-on bridle are followed, except that the head band is butted and nailed touching the nose band, in line with the back corner of the mouth. Just below, through the nose band itself and just above the back corner of the mouth is screwed a screw eyelet for the reins to be attached to.

Removable Bridle

Materials: 23in(584mm) long ⅞in(22mm) wide strap, one 12in(305mm) long ⅝in (16mm) wide strap and one 15in(381mm) long ½in(13mm) wide strap. A minimum of nine rivets and three ½in(13mm) buckles.

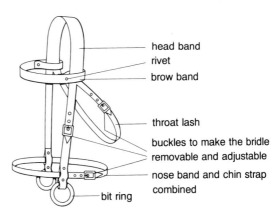

head band

rivet

brow band

throat lash

buckles to make the bridle removable and adjustable

nose band and chin strap combined

bit ring

A removable and adjustable bridle.

To look at, the removable bridle is very similar in style to the nailed-on versions but it is totally different to make (*see* above).

Use the ⅞in(22mm) wide strap for the long head strap that goes from the bit ring on one side of the mouth, up over the head, behind the ears and down the other side of the face to the other bit ring. Allow 2¾in(70mm) turn back on each end, plus an extra 2½in(63mm) on the side that goes down the left cheek. Split equally in two this wide strap from its ends up as far as the temple on both sides, including the extra 2½in(63mm) on the left-hand side. (Left is defined as what would be the horse's left.) This makes two smaller straps of ⅜in(9mm) wide approximately, going down each cheek. The ends of the ⅜in(9mm) front strap on either side go through the bit rings, turning them under and back on themselves for 2¾in(70mm).

> **Tip** With care the length of the brow band can be made to allow the head band to be positioned so that it covers the join between the mane and the forelock and also keeps the headband away from the eyes of the horse.

Make a fastening close to the bit ring with a rivet or stitching and a second fastening approximately 1½(38mm) further up so that there is an open space between the two fastening points. Through this space thread a suitable length of ½in(13mm) strap with a ½in(13mm) buckle fastened to one end and the other end punched with a row of holes so that it can be fitted round the nose and fastened by the buckle underneath, behind the chin, and so forming the adjustable nose band. There should still be a lot of slack on the front strap going down the left cheek; cut this through about half-way up the cheek

and rivet or sew a ½in(13mm) buckle on the lower end; also punch a row of holes in the upper end to make the vertical head band adjustable and removable.

The back free ⅜in(9mm) strap coming down the right cheek is tucked under the throat and half-way up the left cheek, where it is cut off and a ½in(13mm) buckle put on the end. The corresponding back strap coming down the left cheek has a row of holes punched in the end and buckled to the one from the right side, making the throat lash. For convenience the throat lash may need cutting shorter! To make the brow band, the length of

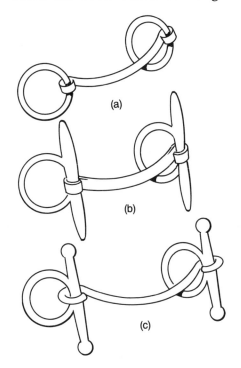

Traditional bits. (a) A simple hand-forged type bit, as used in the early nineteenth century. (b) A hand-forged bit like this one was used in the late nineteenth and early twentieth century on better-quality horses. (c) This type of bit is typical of those used by Triang in the mid-twentieth century.

⅝in(16mm) strapping has one end looped round the head strap at the temple at one side, and back on to itself to be rivetted or sewn in place; the strap then goes across the forehead and is looped round the head band at the other temple and rivetted or sewn in place.

Removable bridles are fun to use and look good on medium and large rocking horses, but the face of a very small horse becomes so cluttered with straps that it almost disappears, so either a modified version using only ½in(13mm) strapping and making the head band and nose band only, or a nailed on bridle of thin leather looks much better.

BIT

Metal bits with a ring at each end (*see* left). A description of different types is given in Chapter 10.

REINS

> Materials: ½in(13mm) wide, ⅛in(3mm) thick and 30in(762mm) long, robust strapping with the options of two swivel clips, four rivets or thread for sewing.

Reins are kept short on a rocking horse because children are inclined to hold them at full length. This means they are sitting too far back, or are leaning uncomfortably back in the saddle if the reins are too long. The ends are looped and rivetted or sewn round the rings of the bit, or through the screw eyelets of the closed mouth bridle. Another option is to have a swivel clip on each end. This is not only extra fun as it means that the reins can be removed at will, but it also keeps the wear down on the weakest spot of the reins, which is where it is fastened at the ends to the bit or screw eyelets. The reins are inclined to break at this point with the constant movement in all directions and the metal clip ends take all this wear instead of the leather.

STIRRUPS

Two 3½in(89mm) across the sole of the foot. Unless a competent blacksmith is available the making of stirrups should not be attempted as the standard of materials and workmanship should be very high for safety, and most sizes for children can be bought quite easily.

MANE AND TAIL

Many different types of materials have been tried from which to make suitable manes and tails, such as rope, wool, fur fabric and nylon, but none looks quite right. It is still horsehair, with possibly the hair from a cow's tail on the smaller horses that helps to give that finishing touch of authenticity. It has been used for the past two hundred years or more and still has not been surpassed. The only exception is perhaps a carved mane and tail, but horses with these are not usually meant for the rough and tumble of a small child's play, more for ornamental display or for the carousel.

Mane

There are three methods that can be used to attach horsehair to the horse's head and neck.

1. The traditional way is to use the skin of a pony's tail. The skin is cured to become hide and the hair is still attached to it. The hide is very stiff and has to be soaked in cold water overnight (twelve hours) to make it soft enough to cut into strips ½in(13mm) to ¾in(19mm) wide, with a sharp knife, from the hide side to avoid cutting the hair. Do not use scissors as cutting the hair is then unavoidable. After the horse has been painted or varnished, the strips are nailed on to the back of the head and neck with 1in(25mm) nails (*see* below), butting the joins down the neck and hiding the heads of the nails in the hair. One short strip is turned with the hair going in the opposite direction and nailed between the ears to become the forelock. The butt join of the forelock to the rest of the mane, if carefully placed, can be hidden under the head strap of the bridle. The base of the mane should end 2in(51mm) to 3in(76mm) above the base of the neck. This allows the hair to flow down the rest of the neck without bunching at the bottom and getting in the way of the stirrups and rider.

> **Tip** To avoid shedding hairs, do not comb or brush the hair until the hide of the pony tail or glue of loose hair is completely dry, which could be a few days.

2. The second way is to use loose horse-hair and fix it in some way so that it can be attached to the head and neck. Long hair 20in(508mm) or more, can be sewn along the centre and glued to a strip of material or leather and nailed on the neck, but long hair is expensive to buy and hair is very slippery, it is much easier to pull out of this type of fixing than it is to keep it in. Also half the length of the hair is hanging in the wrong direction – upside down and therefore will tangle easily and wear out quicker. If combings from a horse are to be used, make sure they are perfectly clean by giving them a shampoo. Glue does not stick to greasy hair. All hair should come from healthy animals.

3. The third way to attach the hair is to use shorter hair, under 20in(508mm) long and glue and clamp ends between two pieces of semi-stiff material such as leather-cloth. This in turn is nailed into the bottom of a ¼in(6mm) wide slot starting ½in (13mm) from just behind the ears to within 2in(51mm) to 3in(76mm) of the bottom of the neck, ⅝in(16mm) deep and cut right down the centre of the back of the neck. Another layer of glue is put in and the gap between hair and slot sides filled with two slivers of wood, or the gaps can be filled

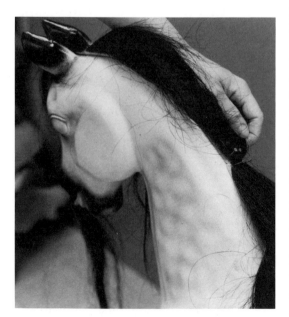

Butting and nailing two pieces of mane on the leather on to the horse's head and neck.

with wood filler. This makes a fairly permanent job, although no mane is completely permanent as children love to comb, plait and generally play with the mane and also the tail, therefore they are usually the first things that wear out. Cut the hair of the forelock shorter than the horse's nose – a horse cannot eat with hair in the way!

Tail

If the horse is to be put on a swinger stand, the tail hair should be short enough not to get fouled up in the swinging mechanism. Tail holes vary in size depending on the size of the horse and the thickness of the tail required. A tail hole $\frac{7}{8}$in (22mm) diameter and 1 $\frac{1}{4}$in(31mm) deep is an average size for a medium horse. Use a spade drill and make the hole in the centre of the rump and in line with the bottom of the neck at a 45° angle to the body (*see right*). It should be drilled after the body has been painted so that the sides of the hole stay clean and the tail will stick in firmly. If the tail hole has to be put in before painting a removable cork will keep the sides clean.

Traditionally a 1½in(38mm) long, slightly tapered, wooden plug was made that was very slack in the tail hole and a piece of the same coloured pony tail that was used for the mane (with long hair attached) was glued and wrapped round the plug and held with one or two tacks. The inside of the plug, piece of pony tail and the sides of the tail hole were smeared with glue, then plug and tail were hammered home with a mallet, the last piece of the plug stuck out into the hair of the tail which gave it 'lift'. Do not be too enthusiastic with hammering in the tail as too

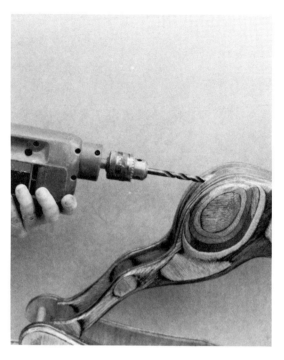

The angle needed to drill the tail hole.

tight a fit may cause the surrounding wood to split. Wipe away any surplus glue that has oozed out.

Another method of making a tail using loose hair is to thoroughly glue and bind it with sewing thread round a 1½in (38mm) long, but small in diameter plug which has a small ⅛in(3mm) hole through the centre of its length. Bind more and more hair on until it is the size of the tail hole. Allow to dry, this might take two or three days as the whole of the end of the tail must be quite stiff. The plug end is then once more smeared with glue and pushed as far as possible into the tail hole. A nail or 2½in(63mm) No. 8 screw is inserted into the hole in the centre of the plug and either nailed or screwed home. Wipe away any surplus glue and leave to dry.

CHAPTER FIVE

MEDIUM HORSE

There is nothing difficult about assembling a rocking horse. Simple joins are used so that anyone with a working knowledge of carpentry and the tools can do it. The skill and interest is in turning the blocks of wood into a three-dimensional horse and stand. A plan which, when made up, gives a good silhouette, helps enormously because nearly all the proportions are already decided, but actually turning this into what is in one's mind's eye takes time, is fascinating and often becomes an all-consuming hobby. The wonderful thing is that it can be done to whatever degree the maker wishes and the type of wood will allow, from a very fine sculpture to just rounding off all the edges. There is always the satisfaction of completion. A child's imagination can always fill in any missing details and whatever the finish, you can guarantee it will be loved.

Most children adore rocking horses. There is something very fundamental about the actual rocking movement. Watch a child's face when they are having a ride. They always look so happy. The medium-sized rocking horse is by far the most popular, as unlike the small horse which becomes too small by the age of five or six years, it is big enough to last a child for most of their childhood yet without being so big that it takes up a large portion of a normal modern-house-sized room, as a large horse is apt to do. It is because of this popularity that the medium-sized horse (in this case 26in(660mm)) has been chosen to describe all the finer detail of carving and assembly.

The instructions are for a fully carved horse on a swinger stand which is the style of the horse most people are thinking of when they are talking of rocking horses from childhood memories. Bow rockers are also included as these are just as popular, and there are other alternative methods and styles of making the horse included where applicable so that the rocking horse can be truly called your own creation. The appearance follows as closely as possible, bearing in mind it is wooden, the lines of a real horse.

The fact that it will get a great deal of hard wear from an unlimited number of children has also been taken into consideration in the design and safety aspect as well as being the type of horse a child would find it fun to own and be able to invent countless games to play with, whether on their own or in a group. Indeed a rocking horse is the ideal toy for an only child as it becomes a companion in play with more 'life' than a stuffed toy because it has movement.

The large horses can be carved and assembled using these instructions for most of the work. Use the charts applicable to get the actual sizes and also follow the extra instructions for the large horse on swinger stand and the large horse on bow rockers.

Before buying the wood and making the horse, as well as the size of the horse, the type of stand should be decided upon. Points in favour of both main types are discussed under 'medium rockers'. All plans of rockers in this book are designed to slide at the end of their rock and not to tip.

DIMENSIONS

On a swinger stand 43in(1,092mm) overall height from the floor, 33in(840mm) to the saddle, 26in(660mm) from breast to rump, 48in(1,220mm) long and 17in(430mm) wide approximately.

On a bow rocker 40in(1,016mm) overall height from the floor, 30in(762mm) to the saddle, 26in(660mm) from breast to rump, 60in(1,524mm) long and 15in(380mm) wide approximately.

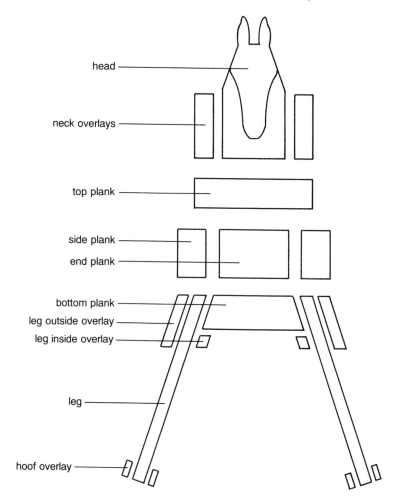

head

neck overlays

top plank

side plank

end plank

bottom plank

leg outside overlay

leg inside overlay

leg

hoof overlay

Position of the pieces of wood used for a medium horse looking from the front.

TIME

Over fifty hours not including time taken for glue and paint to dry.

MATERIALS

Horse

Head: 1 × softwood 10½×17×3in
(267×432×76mm)
Top plank: 1 × softwood 26×8×2in
(660×203×51mm)
Side plank: 2 × softwood 26×4×2in
(660×102×51mm)
End plank: 2 × softwood 4×4×3in
(102×102×76mm)
Bottom plank: 1 × softwood 26×8×2in
(660×203×51mm)
Front leg: 2 × hardwood 1¼in(32mm) thick
– see note
Back leg: 2 × hardwood 1¼in(32mm) thick
– see note
Neck overlay: 2 × softwood 8×6½×1in
(203×165×25mm)
Front leg overlay: 2 × softwood 5×3½×⅜in
(127×89×9mm)
Back leg overlay: 2 × softwood 4×3½×⅜in
(102×89×9mm)
Dowel: 1 × 72in(1,829mm) long by
⅜in(9mm) diameter
Screws: 8 × 2½in(63mm) No. 8 and 4 ×
3in(76mm) No. 10
Roofing bolts: 4 × M6 length to be checked
on finished horse
Eyes glass brown iris: 2 × 1in(25mm)

Rockers

Rockers: 2 × hardwood 1¼in(32mm)
thick – see note
Spacer bars: 3 × hardwood ⅞in(22mm)
diameter by 13in(330mm) long
approximately
Screws: 6 × 1½in(38mm) No. 8

Stand (See Diagram and Chart for Wood)

Wedge: 4 × hardwood size as required
Clamp: 2 × metal to suit ⅜in(9mm)
diameter swinger bar
Swinger bar: 2 × (see diagram and chart
for size)
Cap: 4 × metal to protect swinger ends
Base plate: 2 × metal 3×¼×1⁄16in
(76×6×2mm) minimum size
Screws: 12 × 2in(51mm) No. 8 countersink
Gimp pins: 4 × ½in(13mm)
Nails: 12 × ⅜in(9mm)
Split pins: 4 × (size depends on size of
hole)

Note: Legs and rockers can be cut from the same piece of hardwood 72×14×1¼in (1,830×356×32mm), *or* legs and hoof rails for the stand can be cut from the same piece of hardwood 72×12×1¼ (1,830×305× 32mm).

TOOLS

See Chapter 3. All the tools in List One or their alternatives are needed. Tools in List Two can be used if available and also some of List Three. Please read the lists carefully as it depends whether you are only making one horse or several as to whether it may be worth buying any extra tools.

Bit: 1 × countersink 1⅛in(28mm)
Drills: 1 each × ½in(13mm), ⅜in(9mm),
¼in(6mm), 3⁄16in(5mm), ⅛(3mm)

ACCESSORIES

Except for a mane and tail without which the horse would look unfinished and bald, all accessories are optional and not necessary if the horse is for display only. For a child's use some accessories are needed such as reins, saddle, stirrups and stirrup-straps but others are for decoration giving the horse extra realism and authenticity. On the other hand if the accessories are removable such as the bridle and saddle, apart from the extra fun of 'tacking up' they are a start in teaching a child how to use and look after equipment for when they have to do the same for a real horse. Details of all the types of accessories can be found in Chapter 4.

MEDIUM HEAD

It is assumed that the person making the rocking horse knows the correct way to handle tools and has a certain amount of woodworking skills, but is not an expert at either carpentry or carving, but if in doubt try carving a head out of an odd piece of wood first.

Head Construction

The head can be constructed out of one piece of good quality, well-seasoned softwood 10½×17×3in(266×432×75mm). Alternatively if a solid piece of timber is not available, the same size may be obtained by planing and gluing together two

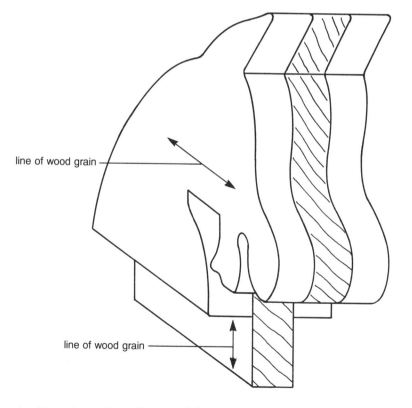

line of wood grain

line of wood grain

A head made of three laminations. (Not to scale.)

12×10×1½in(305×254×38mm) or three 12×10×1in(305×254×25mm) pieces of wood. If three pieces are used to make the head the centre piece of wood should have the grain running vertically instead of horizontally (see page 39) and also elongated at the bottom edge by 2in(51mm) to make a mortice and tenon joint into the top body plank of wood, making a good firm joint. This is only satisfactory with a three-piece lamination as two pieces or one solid piece would have the grain running horizontally to give strength to the ears and therefore a mortice and tenon joint would be weak. The disadvantage of a centre lamination having the grain in the opposite direction is that it is more difficult to carve with a chisel. Detail around the nose, mouth and chin might be better done with a round surform or rifler file.

> **Tip** Drawings and photographs of horses heads will prove useful as they will remind you of the relationship of the features of the head to each other, eyes, nose, nostrils, mouth and ears. A book on how to draw horses can also be very helpful as it will discuss in detail all parts of a horse's anatomy and will give the right proportions.

Head Design

The actual design of the head allows for plenty of scope for individual preference and between the one extreme when the neck and head are stretched out (racer) as if the horse is in full gallop and the other where the neck is arched and the nose pulled well in (jibber) as horses are during dressage.

The head in this plan has the nose pulled in. However, in designing a head there are two important points to consider: first to ensure that the jaw of the head with an open mouth is strong enough to take the pull on the bit, knocks, etc., and second, that the ears are 'pinched' forwards for safety, because as the horse rocks back the child counterbalances by leaning forward and in the event of head to head contact it is important that there are no sharp points.

1. First cut out the silhouette of the horse's head on a band-saw.
2. The back corner of the mouth can be drilled out vertically with a ½in(13mm) twist drill and a small hole ⅛in(3mm) is drilled vertically right through the head to mark the place where the centre of the eyes will be.
3. This also acts as a guide hole for cutting with a spade drill a hole ¼in(6mm) deep and ⅛in(3mm) larger than the eyes to be fitted 1in(25mm). This will allow the 'eye' to be seen at all stages of the carving and help to get the other features in balance.
4. Now more precise lines of the head, the position of the cheek can be drawn in pencil, copying the suggested lines shown on the plan. Draw a line with a flexible tape rule up the centre of the back of the neck, over the ears and down the front centre of the face, through the centre of the mouth, over the chin and end up at the bottom front centre of the neck. This is to help to check that each side is even when carving.
5. The cheek of a horse is very large and flat so first of all the edges need rounding off towards the neck crease and under the throat, but the edge nearest the mouth slopes quite abruptly so that the back of the mouth is at least ½in(13mm) smaller

Tip If you have never done any carving before, use an odd piece of softwood and have a dummy run, then any major mistakes will not have been expensive, and you will be able to tackle the head with more confidence. You might find you have also got an interesting doorstop!

The start of the carving, still showing the pencil guide lines. This head is made of two pieces of wood; the join is just below the ear.

in width than before carving, 2½in (63mm) or less.

6. There is another slope inwards at the top end of the cheek towards the back of the head, behind the ears and again above the eyebrows to the base of the ears so that the thickness of the wood just below the base of the ears is about 2½in(63mm) (*see* bottom right).

7. There is quite a sharp straight dip between the front edge of the cheek-bone and the slender bridge of the nose. In a real

Tip If you are carving with the head flat on the bench, leave the nostrils and part of the lower lip until the last as this will help to balance the wood and when one side of the jaw has been completely carved, slide a piece of wood of the right thickness under the carved side of the jaw when the head has been turned over to carve the other side of the jaw. This will stop any strain on the jaw. The carving of the mouth and jaw should be done very carefully with a freshly sharpened chisel as it is quite easy to knock off the whole jaw if the job is attacked too enthusiastically.

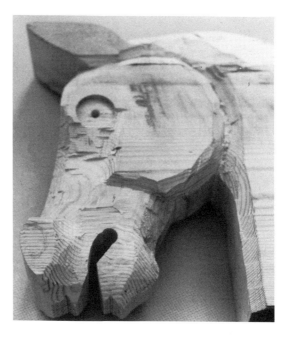

Ready for the nose, ears and teeth to be carved.

horse this allows it to see down its nose when its head is outstretched while in full gallop.

8. Generally the lips are shown pulled back to reveal the teeth and the mouth slightly open as shown in the plan. This gives the mouth more variety and allows the white of the teeth to shine out when the horse is painted and the bit to be inserted.

9. There is a slope from the lower lip that goes under the jaw to the little chin which is also rounded.

10. Where shown on the plan saw with a fine-toothed tenon-saw if possible, a line ¼in(6mm) deep at the base of where the teeth will be and chisel out the surplus wood to form the teeth.

Nose

11. The bridge of the nose of a horse is quite narrow. It is broadest at eyebrow level, narrowing all the way down to end in a V between the nostrils. The edges of the bridge are well rounded – there is a groove right down the centre from fore-head to nostrils.

12. After taking away the surplus wood with a chisel or gouge, most of the mouth, chin and nose detailed carving can be done with a round surform.

13. At rest a horse's nostrils neither point forward nor out sideways, but somewhere between the two, but because they are very mobile there are different positions in which they can be carved. The main three are: one, with a full rounded nostril stand-ing out from the nose as if the horse is breathing hard; this is the favourite posi-tion of the old rocking horses. Two, half open as when trotting, or three, the resting position. Mark in pencil the desired angle of the nostrils which depends on which of the three positions is to be used. Saw off the surplus wood with a tenon-saw.

14. On the two flat surfaces left draw the actual shape of each nostril and then with a small gouge to fit the inside curve, carve out the nostrils to ³⁄₁₆in(5mm) depth. Using either a round surform, or better still, a round rifler file, take away the excess wood from the outside curve of the nostrils so that they stand away from the bridge of the nose and the lips (*see* bottom right).

Tip As it is difficult to sand the in-side of the nostrils or ears completely smooth, put a little dab of wood filler in each nostril or ear and smooth it down with the finger tips.

Ears

15. Draw in a pencilled shape of the ears on their flat fronts. The ears should be as wide apart as the wood will allow. The widest part of the ear is half-way up, being approximately 1⅛in(28mm) across, slim-ming down towards the base which is ⅞in(21mm) and tapering up to the tips which on a real horse are quite pointed, but for safety reasons should be rounded on a rocking horse. Cut a ½in(13mm) slot be-tween the ears with a tenon-saw taking away the waste wood with a ½in(13mm) flat chisel.

16. Start to pare away the wood from the front outside edges with a flat chisel and then do the same on the inside edges. Now the shape of the ears is established, round the backs of the ears with a round surform so that none of the back can be seen when looking square on to the ears from the front (*see* top right).

17. With a small gouge scoop out some of the front of each ear to make it look more lifelike. Do not make these hollows too deep or it will weaken the ear.

18. Tidy up between the ears with a small flat rifler file and sanding paper.

19. Sand the face and ears with a fine disc on a soft-backed sanding attachment on an electric hand drill. Finish by hand sanding ready for painting (*see* below). It is very tempting to put the eyes in at this point, but if they are glass and even more so if they are plastic they are liable to be damaged while the rest of the work is being done. It is better to insert the eyes last thing before painting.

Carved Eyes

20. The eyes can of course be carved, which is more effective when hardwood is used for the head as there will be fine detail to be carved which is difficult to do with a softwood, but not impossible. Small-bladed carving tools would be needed and

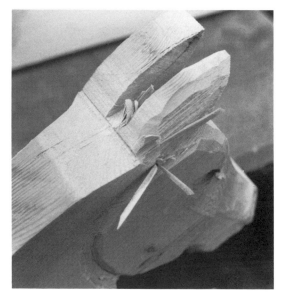

Carving the ear.

The head sanded and neck overlay glued on.

the result, even when an eye is painted on, does not have the sparkle of reality that a glass eye has.

Neck

21. When the features of the head have been carved and sanded ready for painting, the neck overlays can be glued and clamped into position (*see* page 43).

Tip Freshly glued and clamped joins should not have their clamps removed until enough time has elapsed as stated on the glue container. This also applies to cutting off excess wood of wedges and dowels, which should be cut off immediately after or when they are completely dry as otherwise any slight movement may crystallize the glue and it will lose most of its sticking power.

---

22. The back of the head and neck are carved to slope outwards and downwards from the top to where the neck will meet the body.

23. The neck is rounded at the front and back. The sanding of the neck can be left until the horse is assembled, except at the front and under the chin and throat which should be sanded smooth and ready for painting. The sanding of the neck and body, when they are glued together, helps the neck to 'flow' better into the body as there should be no sign of a join when the horse is completed.

24. Some horses show the tendons running from the edge of the upper cheek in a curve down the neck. This is an optional refinement (*see* instructions for the large horse) and should be copied from a photograph, otherwise if this is not done correctly it looks very false.

25. Another refinement is to have the head centred to one side, which is done by making the overlays 1in(25mm) wider and moving one towards the front of the neck and the other to the back. This makes it possible to realign the pencilled line that shows the centre front and back of the neck (the centre line will stay the same over the top of the head, face, nose, chin and top of the throat).

26. Carving is done the same as with a straight neck, but keeping the sides even by the new pencil mark. Eventually when the neck is glued to the body the new pencil marks are used as the centre markings to be aligned with the centre pencil markings on the body and the head will be centred to one side as horses often do hold their heads.

When all the shaping has been completed, plane the bottom of the head flat so that it will be a perfect fit on to the body.

MEDIUM BODY

The body of the horse is the easiest part to construct. It is literally no more than a modified oblong box with butt joins. The carving consists of making this oblong box into a rounded shape, except for the front where there is more detail. There should be no angles; there are almost no straight lines on a horse, so there is quite a lot of surplus wood to be chiselled and sanded away.

1. Make sure that all the pieces of wood to be used for the body are planed and the edges square before starting assembly.

2. Glue the two long and two short pieces of wood together to make a hollow oblong measuring 26×8×4in(660×203×102mm)

which is the middle section of the body. When this is dry plane any unevenness of the upper and lower surfaces.

3. Saw out the leg sockets at each corner of the bottom plank as indicated in the chart overleaf and the line-drawing below.

4. Temporarily screw with 2½in (64mm) No. 8 screws the top and bottom planks to the middle section, matching edges where possible. Use four screws for each plank (*see* overleaf).

5. Mark on the top plank where the head will be, and draw a pencil line along the centre of the plank, down the centre of the back, along the underneath of the bottom plank where the belly will be and up the centre front which will be the breast to meet the line on the top plank. This will help to get a balanced horse by a constant check being kept that both sides are carved alike. When carving be careful to avoid the holding screws or take one out when carving in that area. Screws may have to be

> **Tip** It is much easier and less frustrating to do most of the work on the horse itself in three separate sections, the head, the body and the legs. If the general shaping and some of the sanding is done while the horse is still in pieces, there will be no legs or head getting in the way while carving the body and vice versa.

changed for shorter ones as the wood is carved away.

6. Now the body is ready for carving. The rump is a very good place to begin the carving; there is plenty of scope for shaping as the horse's rump has to look rounded from all angles. Leave the very bottom corners of the middle section uncarved until the legs have been glued in position and the leg overlays in place. It is

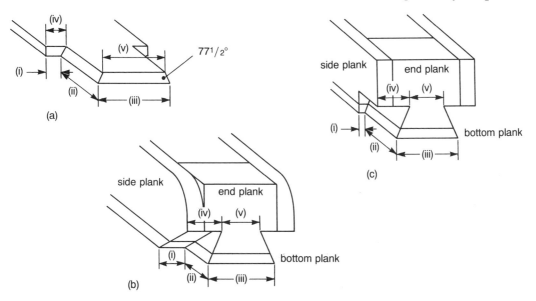

Leg sockets. (a) The bottom plank of tiny and medium rocking horses, and of the large horse on a swinger stand. (b) The front leg socket for a large horse on bow rockers only. (c) The back leg socket for the large horse on bow rockers only.

TYPE OF HORSE	i	ii	iii	iv	v
TINY CARVED	¾in(20mm)	2⅝in(67mm)	2½in(64mm)	15/16in(24mm)	2⅛in(54mm)
MEDIUM	1⅝in(41mm)	5in(127mm)	4½in(114mm)	2⅛in(54mm)	3¾in(95mm)
LARGE ON SWINGER STAND	1⅝in(41mm)	4½in(114mm)	5½in(140mm)	2⅛in(54mm)	4¾in(121mm)
LARGE ON BOW ROCKERS	1½in(38mm)	7½in(191mm)	6½in(165mm)	2¾in(70mm)	4½in(114mm)

Measurements for the leg sockets in the bottom plank of body.

very easy to carve too much away at this point as it is not the bottom of the body. Be careful not to carve away so much at the top of the rump that there is not enough wood left to secure the tail in a 1¼in(32mm) deep hole.

7. At the front, the neck ends in a short V and most horses have an inverted heart shape which goes from between the front legs to about half-way up their breast. This heart shape is not essential but it does give the chance to do some extra interesting carving.

8. In the saddle area from the points of croup (see diagram of a horse) the horse's back slopes down by ½in(13mm) or 1in(25mm) on the large horses towards the bottom of the neck (withers).

The body before carving.

9. From the centre of the saddle area, the sides of the body slope downwards and outwards to half-way down the ribs and then a rounded slope goes inwards ending underneath to form a lovely rounded belly (*see* right). **Note**: If at the top of the legs on the inside, overlays are to be glued then the carving between the legs on the body should not be completed until the position of the finished (carved and sanded) overlays are marked on the bottom plank of the body (*see* below). This will enable the body and legs to flow from one to the other.

10. From the centre of the belly underneath there is a slope of ½in(13mm) up to between the back legs and then this

General carving of the body.

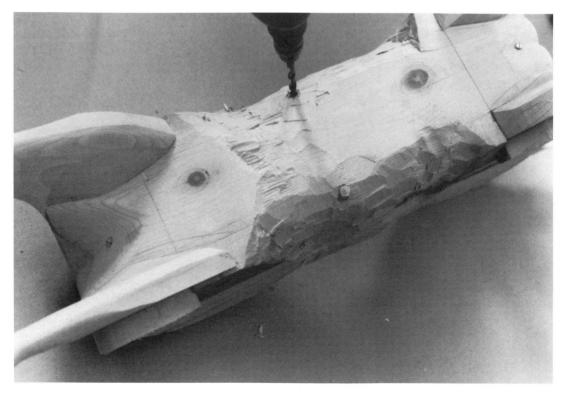

Exchanging screws for dowels. The top inside overlays are shaped, sanded and neatly meet the back groove.

Carving the groove between the back legs.

becomes a groove and as it goes further between the back legs, widens and deepens until it meets the furthest point of where the back legs or their overlays will be (*see* above). The groove then goes up the back centre of the body and starts to narrow and become shallower until it finishes just below the point where the tail will be and just over half-way up the rump.

11. You will notice that the sides of the neck flow straight into the body. The bones of a horse are differently placed to ours, therefore there is no shoulder ridge at the side of the neck, just strong muscles covering a bone that slopes from the withers to a point above the front legs.

12. At this point it becomes a bunched muscle at the top of the forelegs. The rear end of this muscle follows through into the shaping of the ribs as it curves inwards (*see* opposite).

13. There is a similar curving inwards from the muscles just above the back leg to

the ribs. This dip goes right up the side of the horse to the point of the croup.

14. From the centre of the belly and over the chest there is a slight curve upwards just before the start of the forelegs. From about half-way along and between the forelegs there is a gradual slope upwards to meet the bottom of the inverted heart shape with its centre groove or just a short groove on its own.

The above is an indication of the main details of the body carving. There is plenty of scope to add further details of muscles and sinews if you have the time and the inclination.

Alternatives

Instead of an almost flat saddle area to the horse, a wooden backrest for a saddle can be inserted across the horse's back just forward of the points of croup. Details of this can be found in Chapter 10. With the traditional backrest the horse would need the traditional type of saddle (see accessories chapter).

Mortice and tenon joints can be used for the leg joins instead nf sawing out the corners of the bottom plank to butt join. On each corner of the outside of the bottom plank, mark out the mortice ¾in (19mm) from the side and 1in(24mm) from the end. Draw rectangles 3in(76mm) long by ¾in(19mm) wide and parallel with the sides of the bottom plank. Using these rectangles cut mortices right through the 2in(51mm) of the bottom plank, slanting them outwards at 12½° from upright so that when the tenons of the legs are inserted the legs will splay out at the correct angle. *See* Point 3 of 'Legs', page 50.

When carving is complete the body can be left like that until the whole horse is

Carved top of the front leg and bunched muscles.

assembled. The exception is that the area between the legs needs to be fine sanded and made ready for painting as this is very awkward to do once the legs are permanently in position.

MEDIUM LEGS

The rocking horse literally stands or falls on its legs, or more accurately for the maker, its leg joints. The legs not only set the gait of the horse, they provide the support for the rider and it is through the horse's legs that all movement is transmitted. Therefore, while the rocking horse's head gets all the attention, it is the legs that need all the work. Put another way, if the head demands the best of the woodcarver, then the legs are equally demanding of the woodworker.

1. Cutting out the shape of the legs with a band-saw, or its equivalent, will not prove difficult, but a word of warning: of all the timber chosen to make your horse, take the greatest care in selecting the timber for the legs. Hardwood with a good straight long grain, with no blemishes is the best. The legs must be cut along the straight grain of the wood, as indicated on the plans, to give them the greatest strength possible. As an extra, 1/4in(6mm) thick pads the same shape as the hooves and made of softwood can be glued onto the sides to give the hooves a more rounded authentic look. If the horse is going on bow rockers, the rockers need to be made after the legs have been glued to the body, as the rockers are fitted to the legs, but if the horse is going on a swinger stand the hoof rails are made first as the legs are fitted to the hoof rails.

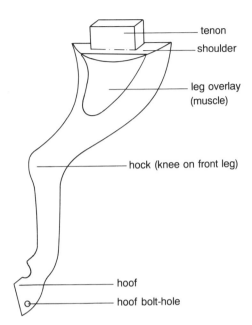

tenon

shoulder

leg overlay
(muscle)

hock (knee on front leg)

hoof

hoof bolt-hole

The traditional way to join the back leg to the horse – using a mortice and tenon joint.

2.   There are two alternative ways of joining the legs to the body. The first method has an open socket sawn out of each corner of the body instead of the traditional mortice and tenon joint. It is a much more positive join as it can be seen if the surfaces are making good contact. The cutting of these sockets are described in the instructions on making the body; the only addition is to angle the top edge of the legs so that they fit snugly into the sockets (see tip in the small horse chapter). This is the type of joint used for all the plans in this book.

3.   The second is the traditional method and an alteration to sfe top 2in(51mm) of the legs shown on the plans would be needed to do this, which is to mark out *only*, a tenon at the top of each leg 3in(76mm) long, 2in(51mm) deep with a shoulder of 1in(25mm) at each end and ½in(13mm) wide along the length on the

outside (*see* left). The mortices must be prepared in a corresponding position at each corner of the base plank of the body instead of cut-outs as described in 'Making the Body'. The angle of the mortice is 12½° to the body, slanting outwards. If this is to be done by hand and not with a morticer, keep checking that the angle is still 12½° while chiselling out the mortice, because even 1° will make a big difference to whether the stance of the horse is crooked or straight. This 12½° spay of the legs is very important as it gives the horse its stability, without looking awkward. Clean the sides of the mortice carefully with a chisel so that there will be good adhesion with the glue when the tenon is put in, and take great care not to exceed the sizes marked on the tenon. Only after the mortice has been chopped out should the tenon be cut. Making the joint in this order will give an opportunity to increase the size of the tenon if the mortice has ended up oversized. Ideally what is required is a firm, hand-tight fit, or one tapped only lightly with a mallet. The tenon must not be forced in otherwise it will split the softwood surround and the whole joint will be weakened.

4.   After the final checks, when the joint has been glued together, for extra strength, two holes can be drilled through the bottom plank, through the tenon and into the bottom plank the other side to a depth of 2½in(63mm) and two ⅜in(9mm) dowels glued in (*see* opposite).

5.   Whichever method is used, at this stage and before any carving or gluing is done, slot in or screw each leg into position with three 2in(51mm) No. 8 screws and check that the horse is standing correctly. Any adjustments can now be made to the legs by shortening the toes or paring small amounts off sockets, top or shoulders. The

maximum wobble that can be adjusted when the rebates are cut in the hooves is about ⅜in(9mm). A spirit level across the horse's back will help to get a perfectly upright position.

6. The hoof rails should be made at this point if the horse is to have a swinger stand. Put the horse on the completed hoof rails to make sure that the hooves fit on the rails and have enough to spare overlapping the outside edge so as not to weaken the hoof when the rebate is cut out. Ideally only half the hoof should be over the hoof rail. Adjust the leg joint, if necessary. Check also that the swinger bars will have plenty of clearance each side when brought up between the legs. If all is well, the legs are unscrewed and carving commences.

Carved legs

7. Like the head and body the amount of detail that is put into the carving of the legs is the maker's own choice, therefore

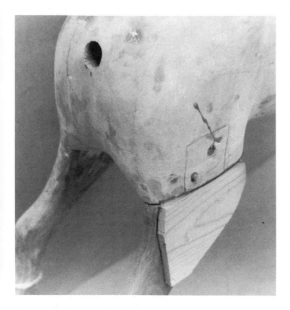

New top of leg overlay and also showing the two dowels put through the tenon to strengthen the joint.

there is only a general indication given here as to where details can be included. Leave the top 4in(102mm) of a leg with a tenon and 2in(51mm) of a plain leg free of any carving. The knee and hock joints are very knobbly and fatter than the leg both just above and below. It is important to note in particular that the back hock is not the same as the front leg knee as it has a depression each side by the point of the hock bone.

8. The lower leg is very straight, but swells out to the fetlock and then narrows quite dramatically for the pastern above the hoof, a point where a straight grain in the wood is very necessary (*see* over page).

9. The rest of the leg should be carved as round as possible and the tendon groove that runs up each side of the back of each leg from fetlock to knee or hock gouged out about ¼in(6mm) deep, leaving the back tendon about ½in(13mm) wide. All the sides of the hooves should be rounded as much as possible, but leave the sole completely flat.

10. There is a further addition to the legs that can be made and that is to put ½in(13mm) thick overlays on the top inside of all four legs where they meet the body and reaching down to about the same level as the overlays on the outside. Chamfer (or bevel) the top edge to meet the body at the correct angle and glue and clamp them in position while the legs are temporarily screwed to the bottom plank. When dry, chisel the edges so that they taper to nothing at all except where they meet the body.

11. Coarse sand and then fine sand the entire legs, except for the part which will be covered by the outside overlays, so that they are ready for painting, this being much easier to do separately than when they are glued to the body. Make the hoof

rails of the swinger stand now if it is to be used.

12. Not until the areas between the front and back leg sockets of the bottom plank of the body have been fine sanded ready for painting are the legs glued and screwed in position, each with three 2in(51mm) No. 8 screws. The bottom plank is immediately unscrewed from the rest of the body in case stray glue from the legs partially sticks the surfaces together. When the glue is dry remove the screws, drill and replace with ⅜in(9mm) dowels.

13. If the horse is going on rockers, they are made at this stage (*see* 'Rockers').

14. The base with legs attached is stood on hoof rails. If you are using rockers the rest of the horse needs to be screwed on so that the correct position on the rockers can be decided, where the horse is balanced

> **Tip** Nick a groove with a chisel along the length of the dowels when they are a tight fit; this lets excess glue escape from where it is being trapped in the end when the dowel is driven home.

equally and not dipping at the front. When the marking is finished the head, top and middle section are unscrewed and taken off. With a 1in(25mm) wide straight edge, mark the position of the rebates on the back, inside and front of all four hooves and saw them out with a tenon-saw (*see* below). This is made easier by having the flat surface of the base plank attached to steady the legs as you saw.

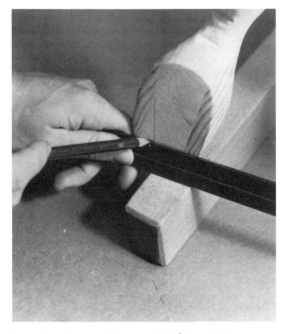

Drawing a horizontal line on the hoof parallel with the hoof rail. This shows also the end of the swinger bar going through the hoof rail.

Cutting out the hoof rebate with a tenon-saw.

15. Screw all the parts of the horse together again and drop onto the rockers or hoof rails to check that the hooves fit with the hoof rails and that the swinger irons will still have plenty of clearance when brought up between the legs.

16. With a ¼in(6mm) drill, drill through the outside part of the hooves that overlaps the sides and through the wood of the rocker or hoof rail beyond, slipping in a bolt every time a hole is made so that the hooves don't move out of position. This is to bolt the horse onto its base. M6 roofing bolts are used, the actual length depending on the size of the rebate that has had to be cut. Partially countersink the heads of the bolts, just leaving enough proud so that the bolts can be removed easily.

> **Tip** The hoof tips are now very vulnerable to being chipped, so using the same hole, bolt an odd piece of wood larger than the rebate on to it, to protect them while the rest of the horse is being finished. This is especially important with the large heavy horses.

BODY ASSEMBLY

1. Now it is the turn of the head. Plane the bottom and clamp it upside down in a vice. Drill four screw holes to take 3in(76mm) No. 10 screws through the top plank, well spaced out and within the area that will be covered by the head. Try the top plank upside down on top of the base of the head and neck, screw into position, dry, drilling pilot holes for the screws if necessary. When satisfied, unscrew, smear on the glue and screw very tightly back into position. Remove the screws when the glue is dry and replace with ⅜in(9mm) dowels. By joining the head and top plank upside down in this way, all the heads of the dowels are within the body of the horse which makes for a neater finish, especially if the horse is to be clear varnished.

2. Before finally assembling the top plank (with head attached), middle hollow section and the bottom plank (with legs attached) check to see if any unevenness has developed between the sections by putting them together without screws.

3. Plane flat any uneven surface and then glue and screw all three sections together. Holding them in sash clamps overnight is even better than just screwing as the joins are held tighter.

> **Tip** To keep the sash clamps from damaging the horse, use two spare long flat pieces of wood or board, putting one piece across and above and one across and below the body of the horse, using the sash clamps to grip either sides of these instead of directly on to the horse.

4. When dry, exchange all the screws holding the body together for ⅜in(9mm) dowels. Be careful when drilling the holes for the dowels that the drill keeps within the wood and does not go in at an angle and so through into the centre hollow of the horse.

5. Draw a line ⅜in(9mm) from the top edge on the outside of one of the front leg overlays and another line on the outside of the top of the other one of the pair. Do the same with the two back leg overlays.

6. In turn lay each overlay on the slanting surface of the bed of the bandsaw (102½°).

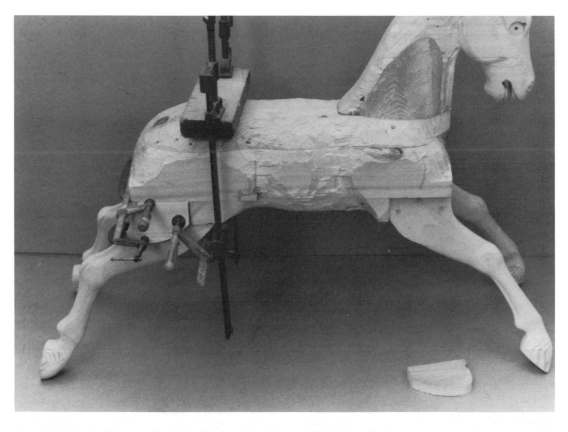

A suggested way of clamping the body of the horse together and the back overlays.

Cut along the pencilled line at the top edge of the overlay taking off a triangular piece of wood. This will quickly give the top edge the right slant so that each will fit exactly over the top of the legs and into what remains of the leg sockets.

7. Glue and clamp all four overlays into position (*see* above).

8. When dry the overlays are chiselled into shape, tapering to nothing the further down the legs the shaping goes. The area at the top of each leg that was left untouched when the carving of the body was done can now be changed into the bunched muscles at the top of the front legs and the graceful curve that flows from body to leg at the top of the back legs.

9. Coarse sand and then fine sand the neck and body, getting the bottom of the neck and the top of the body to flow into each other so that when the horse is painted there will be no visible join. Some wood filler put in at strategic points may be needed to help you, especially if this is your first horse.

10. Before the final sand with the sanding paper on a soft backing, carefully look the horse over for blemishes that need filling with wood filler.

11. Finally sand by hand all over, not only to smooth the areas that cannot be done with any mechanical sanding, but also to give you a second chance to discover any more spots that need wood filler. A good

light is needed for this – sunlight or spotlight; fluorescent is not as good because it is too diffused. The use of an orbital sander for the large areas cuts down time and effort but the last hand sand is very important. If the surface has been skimped it will show up when the horse is painted, especially on the face area (*see* below).

12. The completed horse can now be stood on its hoof rails on rockers. Preparations for the instructions given in point 13 can be made, but the final screwing is not done until the horse is painted and goes on its swinger stand or rockers permanently.

13. A shake-proof nut can be screwed onto the end of the bolt jutting out of the other side of the hoof rail or rockers, or an ordinary nut put on and then a metal cap nailed over for extra protection. Another option is to cut the wood so that the ordinary nut sits in flush. Any excess length of bolt should be cut off and burrs removed for safety reasons.

Eyes

Finally the eyes can be set in to give life to your horse. Probably the most expressive detail of the horse and one job that is comparatively easy to complete if ready made plastic, or better still glass, eyes are used. Glass ones give a more lifelike glint than any others.

Sanded and ready for its eyes.

The important detail to get right is the position. Not only are they approximately a third of the way down the face, taking a line from the base of the back of the ears to the tip of the nose, they are also at either side of the head, not at the front. Remember that a horse in the wild must be able to look ahead and downwards to see where it is galloping and also behind to watch for predators, its eyes therefore are not deep set but stand out from the head a little so that it can have an all-round vision.

There are two different ways of setting eyes into the head. The first is to fill the eye sockets already drilled in the head with

wood filler and whilst this is still soft to push the eye into place with gentle thumb pressure. Filler that oozes out is smoothed away from the eye with the finger tips and later sanded to leave the eye round. When the horse has been completely painted a black line, and sometimes an inner red one as well, is painted in an almond shape round the eye to give it an authentic slant, and traditionally black eyelashes are painted above and below the black liner. All old rocking horses were painted in this fashion from the mid-nineteenth century (*see* below left).

Detail of the finished round eye with almond shaped black liner and eyelashes. Also details of pre-1930s fancy brass rosette and flared nostril.

> **Tip** Glass or plastic eyes with a wire embedded in the back are the best to use as the wire can be cut short and curled into a loop which, when fitted, will embed itself in the wood filler and be an extra precaution against the eye being prized out.

The second method is similar but thumb pressure is exerted only on the bottom half of the eye when pushing it into the socket filled with wood filler, giving the eye a realistic downward slant. The filler that has oozed around the edge is brought just over the rim of the eye and moulded to make eyelids and drawn to the sides into an almond shape. If not enough filler has oozed out, some more may need to be added to complete the lids and surrounds. This gives a much gentler look to the eyes. No painted liners or lashes are used with this type of finish (*see* opposite). If the second method is used on a horse that is to be just clear varnished and not painted, check that the colour of the wood filler matches the surrounding wood *when varn-*

ished or you might have a horse looking as if it hasn't had any sleep for days or resembling an Exmoor pony with its brown coat and pale rings around its eyes as if it is wearing glasses.

The eye surrounds are now ready for sanding. Start with a No. 60 grit and change to a finer one if necessary. Hand sanding is essential for these delicate areas as great control is needed to ensure that the glass or plastic surface of the eyes is not scratched.

The horse is now ready to be painted (*see* page 65).

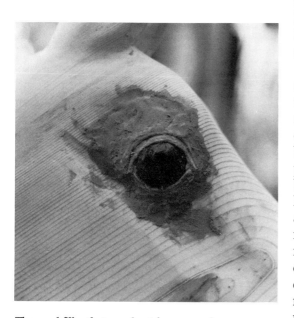

The wood filler that oozed out from around this eye, moulded over the rim of the eye to make lids.

MEDIUM ROCKERS

The choice between making a swinger stand or a rocker is generally a matter of personal preference. A child will be delighted with either. Those who favour the swinger stand, whilst admitting some extra cost and time in construction of this stand, will point out the extra strength and stability of the swinger and also the evenness of the ride. This is an important consideration if the horse is intended to be used constantly by large numbers of children, such as might be found in schools or hospitals.

Those who prefer the rocker will almost certainly do so because of its elegance and period style. It gives exactly the same movement as that of a real horse at full gallop. This can be seen clearly from a slow motion film of a galloping horse. Apart from being less awkward to move around the house, if properly built and properly looked after, the lifetime of a rocker is at least equal if not better than that of a swinger stand.

There are disadvantages of both rockers and swinger stands. Rockers are known as toe crunchers and swingers as shin bashers. Rockers, when they come to the end of their rock, slide along the floor (either backwards or forwards). Stands are supposed to stand still but when the stand becomes worn, a large child can grip the horse between their knees and hump it along the floor making a very satisfying racket! Swinger stands, because they have moving parts, do wear and become loose over a number of years so they will need occasional maintenance. Rockers have no moving parts so there is little maintenance unless the end spacers break away as children are apt to stand on them to get an extra ride.

Rockers

The actual rockers must be of a hardwood as they take the full weight of rider and horse and the underside is in constant contact with the floor, so it gets plenty of wear. Boards if used, and spacer bars can be either the same hardwood or a softer wood, depending on the style chosen. The rockers shown in the plans are for a medium horse and of the simplest style, but they can be adapted to many variations including having the top edge ornately carved, as shown in the photographs of the tiny carved horse, having boards placed across the centre between the two rockers, using thicker rockers or what you will. There are essential points in the rocker design which must be adhered to: firstly that the lower edge of the rockers which are on the floor are smooth and not too steep a curve. Secondly, that there is a flattened area of about 6in(152mm) along the centre bottom of each rocker and thirdly, that the grain of the wood goes correctly along the length of each rocker. The medium rockers are the maximum length that can be cut out in one length; any longer and the rocker must be cut in two pieces or the grain in the wood at the ends of the bow becomes too short which makes it weak enough to crack. The longest grain is always in the centre of the rocker or for the longer ones, in the centre of each of the halves.

1. The plans only show half a rocker so a template needs to be made of a whole rocker before cutting the wood.
2. Cut out the two rocker sides, plane and sand the flat sides, then clamp them together to smooth the inside and outside curves. It is important that the outside curve of both rocker sides are identical with no dents or bumps so that they will give a smooth ride and that the centre of this curve is slightly flattened for 6in(152mm) which will prevent the horse from starting to rock whilst the rider is still mounting.

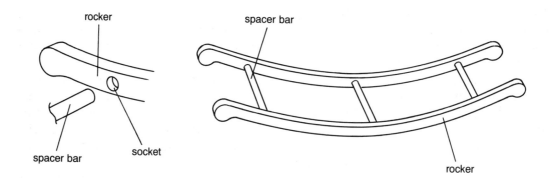

Showing the method used to join the spacer bar and bow rocker together for small and medium horses.

3. While still clamped together, drill ³⁄₁₆in(5mm) diameter screw holes through both rockers where the three places on the plans indicate.

4. Countersink the holes.

5. Mark the rockers in order that there is no fear of turning one round and getting a mis-match. Then unclamp them and on the inside flat surfaces of each rocker enlarge the screw holes with a ⁷⁄₈in(22mm) spade drill to a depth of ⁵⁄₁₆in(8mm) so that they will take the ends of the spacer bars (*see opposite*).

6. Measure between the inside edges of the front toe tips of the horse (ignoring the extra hoof pads if they have been added) and calculate the length of the spacer bar by using this equation: distance between toe tips minus (2 × width of rocker) plus ⁵⁄₈in(16mm). Do the same with the back legs. If there is a difference in measurement then the third central spacer bar measurement is the mean difference between the other two measurements.

7. The three spacer bars can be cut from dowel, or turned, or carved in wood with ⁷⁄₈in(22mm) diameter ends to fit the enlarged holes in the rockers.

8. Glue and screw with 1½in(38mm) No. 8 countersink screws, the spacer bars into their sockets and use a tri-square to check that everything is squared and that the three spacer bars are horizontal.

9. When dry cover the screw heads with wood filler. The rockers are now ready to gauge the hoof rebates of the horse before they are painted or varnished.

The rockers should always be braced in the centre and at either end to give finish to the rocking cradle, stopping any tendency for the legs gradually to spread out sideways with use, which will crack the tops of the legs of the horse.

MEDIUM SWINGER STAND

Top Rail: 1× softwood
48×3½×1¼in(1,219×89×32mm)
Bottom long plank: 1 × softwood
54×4¾× 1¼in(1,372×121×32mm)
Bottom cross plank: 2 × softwood
17×4¾×1¼in(432×121×32mm)
End stop: 2 × softwood
3×4¾×1¼in(76×121×32mm)
Pillar: 2 × hardwood
22×3½×3½in(559×89×89mm)
Hoof Rail: 2 × hardwood 49×2×1in
(1,245×51×25mm)
Wedge: hardwood size as required of offcuts

The hardwood sections plus the legs can be cut from one piece of wood size
72×14×1¼in(1,829×357×32mm).

Clamp: 2 × metal to suit ³⁄₈in(9mm) diameter swinger bar
Swinger bar: 2 × metal road ³⁄₈in(9mm) diameter
Cap: 4 × metal to protect swinger bar ends
Base plate: 2 × metal ¹⁄₃₂in(1mm) thick and ¼in(6mm) to ³⁄₈in(9mm) wide 3in(76mm) long
Screws Countersink: 12 × 1½in(38mm) No. 8
Gimp pins: 4 ×³⁄₈in(9mm)

The swinger stand, sometimes known as a safety stand because it superseded the old very deep Georgian rockers, from which a very vigorous rider could be thrown over the head of the horse in some circumstances, when the horse was at the end of its rock. It is also known as the American rocker as it was an American who first invented this type of stand.

The details given here are for the medium-sized horse, but by using the illustration at the top of page 60 and the chart given at the top of page 61, the sizes can be converted for either the small or large horses.

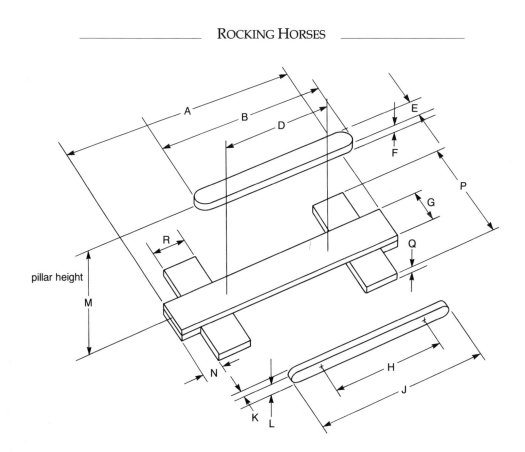

The dimensions of a swinger stand.

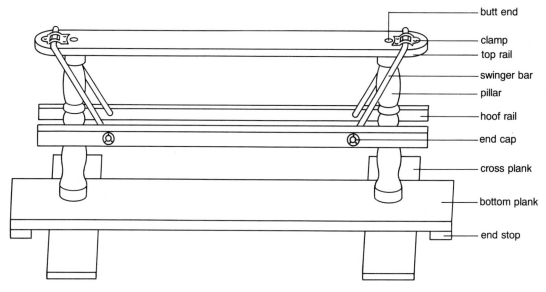

butt end
clamp
top rail
swinger bar
pillar
hoof rail
end cap
cross plank
bottom plank
end stop

The fully constructed swinger stand.

Inches	A	B	D	E	F	G	H	J	K	L	M	P	Q	R
Large	60	54	40	4	1⅜	6	34	51	1	2¼	18	18	1½	5
Medium	54	48	36	3½	1¼	4¾	30	49	1	2	17	17	1¼	4½
Small	44	40	32	3	1¼	4¼	24	40	1¼	2	14	16	1	4

Millimetres

	A	B	D	E	F	G	H	J	K	L	M	P	Q	R
Large	1,524	1,372	1,016	102	34	152	864	1,295	25	57	427	427	38	127
Medium	1,372	1,219	914	89	32	121	762	1,245	25	51	432	432	32	114
Small	1,118	1,016	813	76	32	108	610	1,016	32	51	356	406	25	102

Measurements for small, medium and large swinger stands (see the diagram at the top of page 60).

Base and Cross Planks

The base plank is the plank at the bottom of the swinger stand frame. It is this plank that provides stability, when coupled with the two cross planks. The cross planks must be positioned centrally, under each pillar to give the pillars extra support. As important as the cross planks is the inclusion of a small softwood stop at each end of the base plank, which stops the frame being tipped up by a vigorous rider. They should also be exactly the same thickness as the cross planks.

Pillars

The two pillars can be carved, turned or left square. They should be of a good, well-seasoned, straight grain hardwood and if turned the 'land' at either end should be made slightly concave, so that the pillars seat down on their circumference without rocking. Make sure that the stubs are long enough to go right through the top rail, as well as through the base plank and cross plank together at the other end. If the pillars are to be square take the first diameter measurement in the chart as one side of the square pillar. The ends must be completely flat so that they sit properly against the top and base planks and that the 1¼in(32mm) square tenons are quite central and vertical. They should also be long enough to go right through the top rail and base and cross planks, together (*see* the chart above and the diagram overleaf).

PILLARS

	DIAMETER	EXPOSED LENGTH	TOP STUB		BOTTOM STUB	
			DIAMETER	LENGTH	DIAMETER	LENGTH
SMALL	3in(75mm)	14in(350mm)	1in(25mm)	1½in(38mm)	1in(25mm)	3in(75mm)
MEDIUM	3½in(88mm)	16in(400mm)	1¼in(31mm)	1½in(38mm)	1¼in(31mm)	3in(75mm)
LARGE	4in(100mm)	18in(450mm)	1½in(38mm)	1½in(38mm)	1½in(38mm)	3in(75mm)

Pillar measurements (see the diagram on page 62).

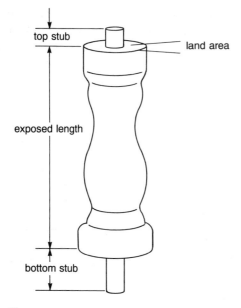

top stub

land area

exposed length

bottom stub

A pillar.

Top Rail

The top plank or rail holds the pillars upright and takes the whole weight of the horse and rider through the swinger bars.

Hoof Rail

The hoof rail keeps the horse rigid and is best made of straight grained hardwood without any blemishes, such as knots. This is because most children use them as a natural step to mount the horse, therefore they have to be very strong, so that they can bear the whole weight of the rider in one small area. If, however, softwood has to be used, the hoof rails should be at least 1in(25mm) more than the normal 2in (51mm) in depth and the holes for the swinger bars, sleeved with metal (which can cause squeaks) or nylon tube. Otherwise the holes wear oval and the swinger bars rattle about, which causes more wear. It can also be unnerving for a timid rider.

Construction

1. Using well-seasoned, good quality softwood, cut out all the planks, plane and round the ends of the top rail. Chamfer the top edges of all items (that is, bevel them symmetrically), except the end stops.

2. Glue and screw with four countersunk 1½in(38mm) No. 8 screws in each of the two cross planks underneath and at right angles to the base plank, central to where the centre of the two pillars will be. Clamp the top rail along the centre of the top of the base plank and equidistant from both ends. Measure and mark the centres of the pillars, 36in(914mm) apart, on the top rail. With a 1¼in(32mm) spade drill, drill two holes for the pillar stubs, right through all three planks (*see* below), or for square pillars, make two mortices 1¼in(32m) square. The holes must be perfectly vertical which will ensure that the stubs of the pillars fit perfectly. Unclamp the planks.

The three pieces of the swinger stand, clamped together so that the hole for the end butt can be drilled right through all three at the same time for accuracy.

3. With a tenon-saw or band-saw, cut V-shaped slots in the stubs or tenons at each end of the pillars. The slots in either end of the same pillar should be cut at right angles to each other so that when the pillars are assembled the slots are at 90°to the length of the top rail and the bottom cross rails, avoiding splitting along the grain when the wedges are driven home. These tapering slots are ready to accept wedges which are made of offcuts of the same hardwood as used for the pillars and are a slightly larger V shape than the slots, but the same width as the stub or tenon. The wedges are cut with the grain going down the V not across it.

4. Using a tri-square, dry assemble all pieces except the wedges, and check for good fit. If the holes for the pillars are too tight, carefully enlarge them with a round surform, rasp or coarse sanding paper, taking care to keep the sides of the holes vertical.

5. Glue and screw with two countersunk 1½in(38mm) No. 8 screws each of the stops to the underside of each end of the bottom plank.

6. Glue pillar stubs or tenons and assemble, checking that they are vertical with the tri-square and that the wedge slots are across the grain of the wood on the top rail. Smear the four wedges with glue and drive home firmly with a mallet, wipe away any excess glue and sand down immediately. Any stubs, tenons or wedges that are left proud cut off, then leave the stand to dry.

Base Plates

The base plates are essential to take the constant wear of the movement of the swinger bars. The best position for them is 3in(76mm) out from the centre line of the pillars, towards the ends of the top rail.

They can be made from sheet metal, which is a minimum of $\frac{1}{32}$in(1mm) thick and $\frac{1}{4}$in(6mm) to $\frac{3}{8}$in(9mm) wide and can be long enough to bend over the edges (in which case check that there are no sharp points or edges) or be just long enough to cover the width of the top rail and held in place with two gimp pins. If sheet metal is not available, two $\frac{3}{4}$in(19mm) No. 8 screws can be carefully placed and partially countersunk, under the swinger bars so that the screw heads take all the wear of the metal bars. This method is more exacting to get right, but effective. A groove the depth of the base plate may need to be cut, with a tenon-saw and chisel, into the top rail.

Swinger Bars

The swinger bars are made from $\frac{3}{8}$in(9mm) diameter, iron, steel, chromed, brass plated or painted rod. Brass rods can be used, but as the metal is softer, there is more likelihood of them being bent out of true if the stand is accidentally knocked over. It is essential that the centre of the U

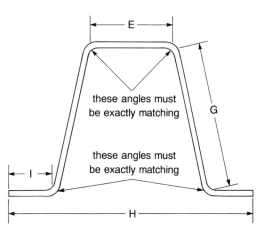

these angles must be exactly matching

these angles must be exactly matching

A swinger bar.

SWINGER BARS

	DIAMETER ROD	LENGTH G	TOP E	BOTTOM H	END I
SMALL	⅜in(10mm)	10in(250mm)	3in(75mm)	11½in(288mm)	1¾in(44mm)
MEDIUM	⅜in(10mm)	12in(300mm)	3½in(89mm)	13in(325mm)	1¾in(44mm)
LARGE	½in(13mm)	14in(350mm)	4in(100mm)	14in(350mm)	1¾in(44mm)

Measurements of swinger bars (see the diagram on page 63).

shape (E) of the swinger bars (*see* diagram) is exactly parallel with the two ends (I) that go through the holes in the hoof rails. If they are not parallel the horse will not swing correctly and there will be wear on the top rail or hoof rail. The swinger bars and the holes in the hoof rails need to be placed correctly to get the best ride possible. *See* the chart above for size.

Hoof Rails

To save expense the two hoof rails can be cut out of the same plank as the horses legs (see appropriate chart). Plane the sides, chamfer the ends and sand away any sharp edges. Drill two ⅜in(9mm) diameter holes 30in(762mm) apart and equidistant from the ends through which to put the swinger bars. The holes can be sleeved with metal or nylon tube, but it is not absolutely necessary as it takes many years for wear to be a problem if good hardwood has been used for the hoof rails. Shortening the measurement between the holes will bring the horse further above the stand and it will buck and shy more steeply when rocked. The easiest way to fix the swinger bars to the hoof rails is first to drill a ¹⁄₁₆in(2mm) diameter hole through at ¹⁄₁₆in(2mm) from the ends of each bar. Put the bar ends through the holes in the hoof

rails and slip on a washer, then secure a split pin through the holes at ends of the bars. Cover this with a metal cap for safety. Another method is to put the washer on the end of the swinger bars after they have been inserted through the holes in the hoof rails, then peen over the ends of the bars, rubbing off any sharp edges. With this method care has to be taken that the swinger bars are not hammered out of true while the peening is done.

Clamps

The swinger bars are held on the top rail by means of a metal bracket or clamp (*see* opposite). As they take a great deal of strain the whole time the horse is in action, the clamp needs to be very strong and a good fit, therefore they are usually purpose made of ⅛in(3mm) cast or pressed iron or brass with a depression across the middle that exactly fits the swinger bar. These are held on to the top rail by M6 bolts or a combination of screws and bolt. Hardwood clamps can be made, but to make them strong enough they have to be thick, which makes them rather bulky (*see* far right). Another way is to weld a metal tube of the right size and thickness to a square plate. The rod is then threaded through and the clamp so formed is ready

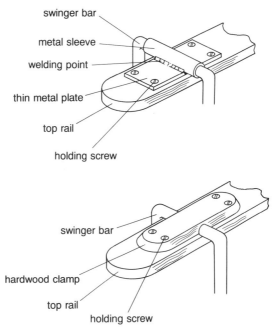

Two alternative ways of clamping the swinger bars to the top rail.

The ends of the two stands, the top stand showing the clamp and base plate. The lower stand has the swinger bar in place both at the top clamp and through the hoof rail with a protective cap nailed over the end. The wedge of the pillar stub is shown going across the grain of the top plank.

to screw or bolt to the top rail. The biggest disadvantage of this is that it has to be in place before the rod is bent to make the swinger bar. Before final assembly of this part of the stand, check that the bar and clamp fit snugly without movement, on to the top rail, yet gives free movement of the bar. The stand is now ready for painting or varnishing and the assembly of the whole rocking horse.

FINISHES

There are three main ways of finishing a rocking horse: painting, varnishing or polishing.

Painting is the most popular with the children as the horse can be made to look near to the colour of a real horse. In a quick survey at an exhibition, all the children who showed any interest, which was most, were asked which horse colour they liked best out of a group of plain wood and painted ones. Nearly every child pointed to the dapple grey among the painted ones. In different countries this preference may change. For instance in some European countries they are very fond of black horses.

Painting is also very popular with first-time makers as blemishes can be filled with wood filler, the colour of the wood is not important and the final effect is pleasing.

Varnish, especially clear, can look very dramatic on a plywood laminated horse as it will show up every swirl of the wood sharply. Clear varnish is also the one to use on a horse that is all of hardwood or carefully matching woods as it will show up the colour and grain of the wood which would be a shame to cover. A sure hand and good joinery are needed for this to be a success. A very hard durable varnish such as polyurethane is the best to use if the rocking horse is to have plenty of use and is constantly in contact with shoes. Polishing is not recommended for a horse that will have hard wear, otherwise it will be a constant job for the owner to keep the shine. It is usually only used on horses that are in the plain hardwood and are only for decoration. The preparation and actual polishing is an art in itself. There are many types and many books on the subject, therefore the suggestion is that the instructions on the polish containers are followed or a book on the subject is consulted.

The finish always reflects the preparation underneath, of which there can be one or two final stages. In other words, gesso can be used on horses that are to be painted, or the horse can be just fine sanded, which is suitable for all three types of finishes.

Gesso

From the middle of the eighteenth century to half-way through the twentieth century gesso was used on nearly all fully carved rocking horses made solely from wood, and is still used on a great many new horses and very often on the restorations of the old ones.

Gesso is white plaster made of a powder mixed with an animal glue, the latter being made from rabbit skins. Used originally by artists as a thin layer to dress a canvas before painting in oils, it was later used in the moulding surround of ornate picture frames that were so fashionable in the nineteenth century. When the carving of a rocking horse is complete and had been roughly sanded, three coats of gesso were put on before the horse was painted. This made a layer of up to $\frac{1}{16}$in(2mm) thick and gave the horse an exceptionally smooth finish. It was also useful as a stopper for resin that might ooze from the knots in the pine by absorbing the resin and therefore stopping it from seeping through the paint. Something else that may not have been realized at the time is that rust does not affect gesso, so rust marks do not show through the paint either. Many horses, especially during the great boom time at the turn of the twentieth century were not well made, inasmuch as they were being turned out so fast and without our technical advances in tools that the workmanship was not always of the best, so gesso was very good for filling in any gap in the wood and covering mistakes.

Early nineteenth-century makers must have been very fond of gesso because not only did they cover the horses, but many of the big old boat-shaped rockers had a layer of gesso coated on to the actual rockers under the green paint, possibly used instead of the primer paint we would use today! There are different qualities of gesso depending how much of the rabbit skin glue has been added. With some makers gesso was very hard and has worn well, but with others, especially around the 1960s, the gesso was soft and chips off quite easily, especially if it has got damp.

Damp affects all gesso as it is water soluble, although to keep a gesso-coated horse at its best, some dampness in the atmosphere is needed. This is clearly shown in the way horses from unheated houses crack when put into centrally-heated ones.

There are some problems when using gesso. The foremost is that it is mixed up with water to make a paste for use, so after the maker has been careful to use dry wood to make his rocking horse and kept it in a dry atmosphere, or dried it out when it was complete, this layer of very wet paste is put on.

Although most of the water dries out into the atmosphere, much of it must also be absorbed by the wood and undo all the good intentions of the maker. A sealer can be painted on before the gesso is applied, but the gesso does not key in very well and is inclined to drip off. A mixture of 33 per cent less water is much better; it makes the coating of gesso very thick. Even this does not stop some of the water from being absorbed into the wood. Unless gesso dries very slowly, it cracks, and then all the cracks have to be filled in with more gesso. Another disadvantage with gesso is that after carefully carving a horse, covering it with three coats of gesso can blunt the finer details of what has been carved, especially on the face, because it makes a thickish layer. In play a rocking horse gets quite a pounding from shoes, stirrups and an assortment of other hard objects and gesso is inclined to chip, which shows up very white under the paint. A similar mark done on painted wood is not so noticeable and in many cases a dab of paint will cover up the mark. Using the type of plastic filler used on walls to fill in where gesso is missing is not very successful as it is a different mixture and not nearly as fine.

Tip Gently tap an area of gesso that is suspected of being loose with the fingernails. If loose, it will give a hollow sound when compared with an area you know to be firm.

Application

Gesso can be difficult to apply if the instructions for making it are not followed exactly, as all the glue must be dissolved or the gesso will be thin and watery, go lumpy or stay powdery when dry. The glue can be bought in slab or sheet form, but the best for making gesso is to get it in granulated form. If you are using sheets or slabs, the glue needs cracking up as small as possible so that it will dissolve in the water easily.

Dissolve ¾oz(38 grams) of glue in ¾pint (450ml) of very hot but *not* boiling water, preferably using a heavy-based saucepan over a low heat. Stir well until all the glue is dissolved. Add 7oz(198 grams) of the whiting and stir in well, apply on to the horse with a 2in(50mm) clean paint brush or soft sponge. Work well in to make an even coat that is as smooth as possible, keeping the mixture warm all the while over a container of hot water to ensure the mixture does not start to set. Allow to dry slowly and sand gently away any lumps with a medium paper. Add two more coats of gesso in the same manner. Give a final sand to ensure complete smoothness. The horse is now ready for painting. The amounts given here are for a large to medium horse. Use 66 per cent of the quantities for a small horse.

To stop any excess mixture that is to be used for the next application from drying out, put a wet cloth over the container, store in a cool damp place and reheat prior to using. Gesso will only keep for a short time in a moist state before it goes bad.

Sanding

This is a very dusty job, therefore it is advisable if at all possible, to do all the sanding in the open air if the work area has no dust extractors. The use of a dust mask is also advised as wood dust can be the cause of chest infections.

The final sanding is done by hand. A good light is essential to see lines left by machine sanding. It is tedious but is worth every minute of the time spent sanding by hand to get all the small difficult corners cleaned out and the large areas really smooth. Hurry this stage and it won't matter how many coats of paint are put on, especially black, the blemishes will show through.

Tip If a cintride disc gets gummed up with resin from the knots in the wood, place it in a bowl and pour boiling water over it. This will quickly loosen all the resin and sawdust.

Now that all the sanding is complete, if there is any doubt at all about the wood not being dry, because of being in a damp atmosphere, put the whole assembly somewhere where it can dry out slowly, for up to two weeks.

Painting

Only paints and varnishes suitable for children's toys should be used. For both a painted horse or a clear varnished one, the first coat is a sealer. When dry this sealer raises the rough end grains and these can be sanded smooth. Then give the whole horse a light sand with a grade 80 sheet of garnet or similar paper. A second sealer is now applied and again lightly hand sanded. These two sealers through absorption into the wood help to stop water absorption and therefore the movement of the wood. They also stop any seeping of resin from knots. Clear varnished horses are now painted with the first coat of varnish and sanded when dry. Further coats of varnish are painted or sprayed on, and the horse is sanded in between with finer sanding paper each time until the desired effect is achieved. This can be up to fourteen coats.

Tip When painting the horse it is easier to do its underside, insides of the legs and under its chin first, then stand the horse on its hooves to complete the rest. In this way it is possible to do a whole coat with minimum of handling.

For painted rocking horses a layer of primer paint is put on, followed by a final check that there are no blemishes that need wood filler. If blemishes do need covering, scrape the paint away at these points so that the wood filler will key in properly. Sand very lightly with very fine paper.

There are now very fine papers made especially for this kind of light sand. Undercoat with the appropriate coloured undercoat to match whatever coloured top coat is to be used. Paint with top coat. If this is to be dappled, it can be either a gloss or a matt finish. For a colour that needs no extra painting the last coat needs to be a paint that gives a good hard finish as it will be in contact with little shoes and constant stroking of little fingers for years.

Dappling

Traditionally the rocking horse and rockers were painted. The horse was almost always painted a blue-grey background with patches of dapple and finished with an overall clear varnish that went yellow with age. The rockers were painted a dark green. Now, however, the more common practice, and certainly an attractive one, is for the horse to be painted white with much more dappling put on and the rockers/stand to be left a natural wood, protected with clear varnish.

Eighty-five per cent of all painted wooden rocking horses that are now made are dappled. Dappling is a painted black and white mottled effect and there are a number of ways of doing it, depending on the equipment, density of dappling required and maker's choice. Some practice is needed for nearly all the methods if never attempted before. Any spray that is used must be compatible with the top coat of paint, e.g. enamel paint needs enamel spray. If this is not done, and for instance an enamel paint is used for the top coat on the horse then a cellulose spray is used, and when the spray dried it would begin to peel off. All types of dappling should be finished with a coat of clear varnish, polyurethane being the best.

1. Finish the coats of white gloss paint and when that is dry, using a small piece of sponge, dip it into black gloss paint and dab small circles of black onto the body, letting the circles fade as the paint on the sponge is used, then starting the process all over again. This fading gives a pleasing effect as a horse does not have the same depth of dappling all over.

2. The same method as above but with a small stippling brush. This was the first way that dappling was put on rocking horses in the middle of the nineteenth century. It needs a lot of patience as unless you are very practised it can take a considerable time, but the effect can be very good, the dappling being either heavy or light as required.

3. A quick, easy method, which looks cute on a small horse is to stick on little rounds of paper (price labels) in strategic areas when the top white coat of paint is dry. Then with a can of black spray give a very light spray of paint over the rounds of paper. When the spray is dry remove the paper rounds. Very effective if only done on the rump, neck and muscle above the forelegs (*see* below).

4. After the top white coat is dry, spray the areas to be dappled very lightly with a can of black spray to give a misty effect, then when this is dry spray little spurts of

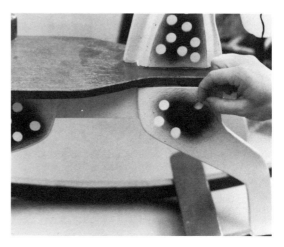

Removing the paper circles after spraying over them.

white on top of the black. This looks quite close to the real thing and is a reasonably cheap way of doing it if only one horse is to be made. However, it needs practice on an upright surface because if the white spray can is too close, the dots of white will have too much paint and will drip. If the can is too far away, there will be only a mist of white and not a distinct dot.

5. With an airbrush and diluted black paint (as instructions that come with the airbrush describe), spray small circles of black paint over all or part of the horse. This gets nearest to the dappling on a real horse as the variation of depth and size of the dappling can be so easily controlled.

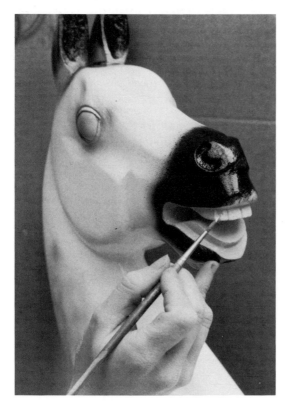

Painting the white teeth. The mouth is pink. Removing paint from the eyes is left until the very end.

6. Finish over the dappling with a coat of varnish.

Traditionally all dappled horses have black ears and noses, black hooves and black on their knees and on their hocks.

Other Colours

There is no reason why a rocking horse cannot be any colour, but here is a list of some colour combinations that occur naturally in horses.

Piebald: Black and white patches, very easy to paint.
Skewbald: Brown and white patches, also easy to paint.
Bay: Brown with black tail and mane.
Dun or Sorrel: Cream with black mane and tail.
Roan: Grey-white or chestnut-white with matching mane and tail.
Brown: Chocolate brown with same mane and tail.
Black: Black with usually some marking of white somewhere.
Chestnut: Chestnut with matching mane and tail.
Palamino: Golden with cream mane and tail (might have to mix your own paint but easy to do).
Appaloosa: White with small black spots or occasionally brown spots. Some spots surrounded by an outer grey circle. Not easy to do without an airbrush.

Brown paint is very difficult to get looking natural, as it is lustreless, so for all-over colour can be very disappointing.

Many horses which are plain coloured have white markings down their noses. These markings fall into four main categories.

Star: Which is a roughly star-shaped marking on the forehead.

Flash: This white mark starts on the forehead and goes about half-way down the nose.

Blaze: Again the white mark starts on the forehead and goes right down the nose, making the front of the upper lip and sometimes under the lips to the chin, white too. Some pink shows around the lips in most cases.

Snips: Small white marking between the nostrils.

Most but not all plain coloured horses have at least one white sock, the sock being all or some of the area from the hoof up to the knee or hock. Very often all four legs have white socks. Black Beauty from the famous children's book of that name was a black horse with a white star and its left foreleg had a white sock.

Antiquing

Some people do not like their rocking horse to look too new. The most uncomplicated way of ageing a horse is to give a large group of children free access to play on it for a year or two!

There are also other ways of taking away the newness of a rocking horse much more quickly. The simplest is to use a clear matt finish that has a trace of light oak varnish in it. The resulting slightly yellow mixture may have to be thinned so that it shows no streaks when it is brushed on, in which case two coats should be painted on. The varnish on an old horse goes dull and yellow so this type of finish simulates it very well. Faking wear marks can be done by rubbing with a fine wire wool, points that usually show wear first such as the outer edges of the ears and hooves, the rump, nose and shoulder muscles, also each side of the mane just behind the ears. Scuff the leather saddle back with a wire brush. Further distressing can be done by putting sharp stones in an old sock and hitting the swinger stand or rockers with it to add small dents. Pay special attention to the top of the back legs where a good rider would naturally kick the horse with their heels when starting a ride. Care should be taken over how hard the horse is hit or it might end up aged to such an extent that it will need restoration! Scuff the edges and corners of the stand or rockers with a coarse file. Use brass domed nails that have been dulled or ones with an antique finish to nail on the saddle and bridle and if a saddle cloth is included, leaving it in strong sunlight to slightly fade the colour before fitting will age it.

These are all the main finishes currently in use. No doubt there are others for individually designed rocking horses, that have the same pleasing effect.

The patterns for the medium rocking horse are on pages 72–3. (Scale 1:4.35.)

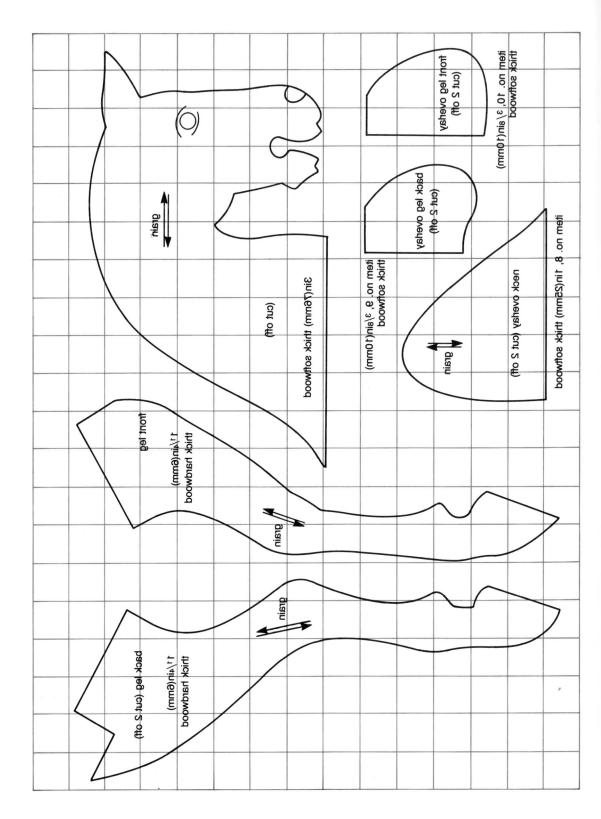

front leg overlay
(cut 2 off)
item no. 10, 3⁄8in(10mm)
thick softwood

back leg overlay
(cut 2 off)
item no. 9, 3⁄8in(10mm)
thick softwood

neck overlay (cut 2 off)
item no. 8, 1in(25mm) thick softwood

grain

3in(76mm) thick softwood
(cut off)

grain

front leg
11⁄4in(6mm)
thick hardwood

grain

back leg (cut 2 off)
11⁄4in(6mm)
thick hardwood

grain

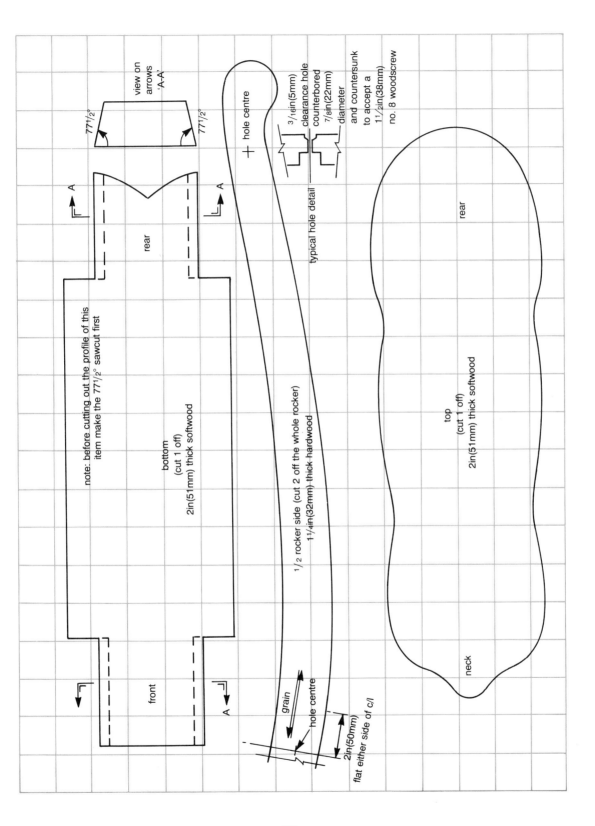

view on arrows 'A-A'

77 1/2°
77 1/2°

+ hole centre

3/16in(5mm) clearance hole
counterbored 7/8in(22mm) diameter
and countersunk to accept a
1 1/2in(38mm) no. 8 woodscrew

typical hole detail

A

rear

A

note: before cutting out the profile of this
item make the 77 1/2° sawcut first

bottom
(cut 1 off)
2in(51mm) thick softwood

front

A

A

1/2 rocker side (cut 2 off the whole rocker)
1 1/4in(32mm) thick hardwood

grain

hole centre

2in(50mm)

flat either side of c/l

top
(cut 1 off)
2in(51mm) thick softwood

rear

neck

CHAPTER SIX

DOLL-SIZED HORSE MADE FROM PLYWOOD

This is a fun horse, strong enough for older children to use as a toy horse for their dolls and yet if it is left in the plain wood and clear varnished, stylish enough to have as an ornament. The horse needs no carving at all with chisels. The only time a chisel is used is to make a slot for an alternative way of fixing the mane. Skill and a gentle touch using sanding discs attached to a hand-held electric drill will do 90 per cent of the shaping. Because the shaping is done quickly, the whole rocking horse can be made in a few hours. The longest processes are waiting for the glue and paint or varnishes to dry. A very satisfying result for a minimum of effort and skill and so pleasing to the eye.

DIMENSIONS

Standing 16in(406mm) high 28in(711mm) long and 4¼in(108mm) wide.

TIME

Approximately ten hours spread over a period of four to five days in order to allow for the drying of the glue and the paint/varnish.

TOOLS

Band-saw or fretsaw, or the equivalent. This is a must as the shapes need to be cut accurately, especially round the face and nose
Electric hand drill with sanding attachments, including a 5in(127mm) diameter rubber backing disc and a smaller soft backing disc
Coarse sanding disc, which can be a cintride for the large backing disc
A fine disc for the smaller soft-backed attachment
1 × ⁷⁄₁₆in(11mm) 1 × ⁵⁄₃₂in(4mm) and 1 × ½in(13mm) twist drills
A countersunk bit
A power file is useful, but not absolutely essential. A flat rifler file can be used instead
Pencil and scissors
Medium screwdriver
5 clamps for each side of the body is the minimum and all 5 must be large enough to clamp 4¼in(108mm) thick wood, the rest (if used)to clamp 2½in(63mm) thick wood
¼in(6mm) or ⅜in(9mm) flat bevel chisel and mallet (only needed if the alternative way of slotted in method of fixing the mane is used)

74

MATERIALS

1 piece of ¹¹⁄₁₆in(18mm) thick by 24in(610mm) wide by 40in(1,016mm) long good quality plywood
1 pair of ³⁄₈in(9mm) glass eyes
Approximately 12in(305mm) of ½in(13mm) diameter dowel
4 × 1in(25mm) No. 6 countersunk screws
Wood glue
Wood filler
Material for mane and tail, such as loose horse or cow hair, horse or cow hair on the leather, fur fabric or wool
12 ½in(13mm) gimp pins if hair on the leather is used
Latex glue for the mane and tail
2 strips 6in(152mm) long and 1in(25mm) wide of thin material such as cotton lining if an alternative method of fixing the mane is used
1 sheet of medium sand paper and 1 sheet of fine sanding paper for hand sanding
Sealer and varnish or paint

CONSTRUCTION

1.   Cut out two combined body and heads, but do not cut out the mouth. Two combined body and legs, two rockers, two rump pads, two belly pads and two shoulder pads.
2.   Glue one combined body and legs onto one combined body and head, matching the edges, also glue onto the body and legs side, one rump pad, one belly pad and one shoulder pad (see overleaf), taking care that all the pads are in the right positions indicated on the plans, as they will form the muscles of the horse. All these parts can be glued and clamped at the same time.
3.   Using the opposite side of the other combined body and head, glue onto it the second body and legs and the other set of pads. When eventually the two combined bodies and heads with the other pieces attached are put together they make a complete horse but *do not* fix the two halves together at this stage.

Tip To make the next stage of sanding easier, temporarily screw an odd square of wood to the middle of the inside of each half of the body. This can be clamped in a vice which will keep the work still while it is being sanded.

---

4.   When the glue is dry on the two halves of the horse, drill a hole in each hoof as indicated on the plan ⁵⁄₃₂in(4mm) diameter to take a No. 6 screw. Countersink the hole on the inside of each hoof.
5.   Drill a ⁷⁄₁₆in (11mm) diameter hole ¼in(6mm) deep in the outside of each half of the head for the eyes. Mark in the guide lines on the head, body and legs with a pencil.

Sanding

6.   With a coarse disc sand off the top two layers of plywood from the pads as they are too thick. Sand down the edges of the pads so that they slope towards the main body and show off all the layers of plywood. Follow the contours of the pads and make the slope as gradual as possible, except towards the front legs, where it should round quite abruptly to show that the muscle is bunched at the lower end of the shoulder.
7.   Sand the outer edges of the rump, belly and neck of the main body so that they meet the pads and show up the colours in the layers of plywood.

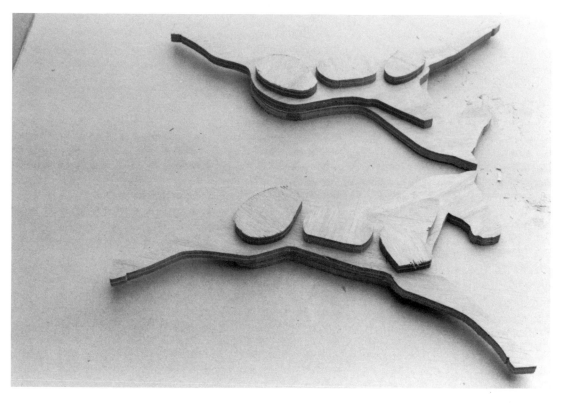

Two halves of the horse with pads in position.

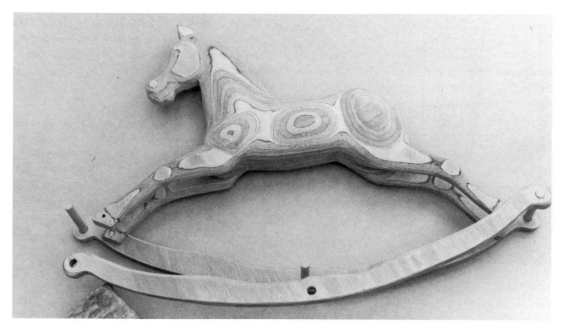

The horse is complete except for the eye. Assembling the rockers.

8. Sand the legs round both inside and outside except for the outsides of the hooves. Just one layer of plywood is sanded away on parts of the sides of the legs above and below to emphasize the knees or hocks.

9. Leave the cheek flat and untouched, but round the edges of the face towards the throat, neck and ears. Scoop away some of the plywood between the cheek and the bridge of the nose, also between the cheek and nostrils (*see* right).

10. The chin, behind the chin and both upper and lower jaw need narrowing and gently curving round. The final shaping of the head can be done when the two halves are glued together (*see* opposite, below).

11. When all the coarse sanding that can possibly be done is finished on the outside of both halves, turn them over and sand the two areas on the body, as indicated on the plans, which are: sanding up between the back legs to give some form to the rump. This needs to be done carefully and exactly the same amount taken away on both halves so that they meet perfectly when glued together and a very small amount of the edge is sanded off between the front legs to make a groove between the two halves in the same place as horses have a groove.

Head, mouth and eye details.

Tip The ears are the most vulnerable part. If the horse is to be painted instead of varnished, a thin coat of glue smeared over each ear will help stop little pieces splintering away.

---

12. Fill in with wood filler any misses between the layers of plywood and where the splinters have come off.

13. Sand one layer of plywood off the inside of the ears. Change to a fine sanding disc on a soft backing. Sand and shape the ears, keeping the fronts flat and rounding the back, curving the sides, but making sure there are no sharp edges. Each ear should stand apart when the two halves are glued together.

14. Soft sand the legs all round and the two interior patches at the back and front of the body also down the back of the neck from head to withers (saddle area). If an alternative method of attaching the mane is to be used by slotting it between the two halves of the neck, then it should be done before the two halves are glued together. (*See* 'Manes', page 79.)

15. Glue and clamp the two halves together, matching edges. When the glue is dry fill in any misses in the plywood and any other patches that need it with wood filler.

Mouth

16. Put on blocks the underside of the head so that when the horse is laid on its side, the head stays horizontal. Cut out the mouth with a band-saw. The mouth is left until now so that it will be cut out in one piece as it would be difficult to remove any unevenness in such a small mouth if done before the two sides were glued together.

17. Soft sand the whole horse, giving particular care to the area around the nose. The area under the chin and throat can be sanded with a power file or rubbed with a rifler file and sanded by hand.

Rockers

18. Clamp the two rockers together, matching edges. With a coarse disc, round the two top outside edges and the curls at the end to show three layers of the plywood. Change to a fine disc and smooth the rounded top edges, the top and bottom of the rockers and just enough of the bottom edge to take the roughness and any splinters off.

19. Where indicated on the plan drill three ½in(13mm) diameter holes right through both rockers, while they are still clamped together. Take the clamps off and smooth the inside edges of the rockers, just enough to take off the roughness.

20. With 1in(25mm) No. 6 screws, screw one rocker on the outside of two hooves checking that the tips of the hooves do not go beyond the bottom edge of the rocker and that they are 1in(25mm) nearer the back end of the rocker than the front.

21. Hold the other rocker in place on the outside of the other two hooves. Measure the distance between the outside edges of both rockers (4in(102mm) approximately). Measure and cut the dowel in three pieces to fit the space between the outsides of the rockers.

22. Glue the three dowels into place in the rocker that is already screwed to the two hooves. Put glue around the opposite ends of the dowels and drop the other rocker on to them, then screw the remaining two hooves on to the inside of this rocker. Sand off any surplus dowel and allow to dry. An alternative to the dowels for the rockers would be to turn three wooden spindles to use in their place.

Eyes

23. Fill the eye sockets with wood filler. Curl over the end of the wire to make a loop at the back of each glass eye and push the eyes into the soft wood filler. Wipe away any surplus wood filler that oozes out. By curling over the wire at the back, the loop gets embedded in the wood filler and makes the eye extra secure from being prised out by little fingers. The other option is to paint the eyes on, painting the same type but very much smaller ⅜in(9mm) as the eyes shown in the photograph of the toddler's rocking horse.

Painted on details of eye, mouth, nose and mane.

24. Cover the four screws in the feet with wood filler, check the whole horse and rockers for anything that needs wood filler and then soft sand or hand sand. The horse is now ready for painting or varnishing.

Finish

25. With all the swirls of the muscles showing well in the plywood, the obvious finish is to clear varnish. In which case, coat with two layers of seal first. If the mane is to be glued on leave a 6in(152mm) long by ¾in(19mm) wide strip from behind the ears down the back of the neck and a little ¾(19mm) strip in front of the ears, of bare wood, so that the mane will stick on better, hand sanding all roughness off thoroughly between each coat. If a painted mane is to be done, paint it before the last coat of varnish is applied. Follow with a minimum of two coats of clear varnish, lightly sanding in between each coat with a fine sanding paper. The more coats of varnish applied, the glossier the horse will become, but do give a light sand in between each coat so the next coat will key in properly, using finer and finer sanding paper for each coat and the surface will become smoother with each sand.

26. The alternative is to paint. Apply first two coats of sealer, sanding away any roughness between each coat and then apply one coat of primer. One or two undercoats are applied before the top coat is put on in your chosen colour or colours. If a mane is to be painted on it is brushed on at the very last. (See chapter on painting and finish.)

Manes

27. There are quite a few alternative ways of making the mane. The quickest is to paint it on, not forgetting to paint the forelock.

28. The glued on method where a piece of fur fabric or something similar 6in(152mm) long by ⅝in(16mm) wide for the mane and a little ¾in(19mm) by ⅝in(16mm) wide forelock are glued on to the bare patches can look very effective for an ornamental horse, but would not stay put for so very long if the horse is to be used for play.

29. The same sized piece as the fur fabric of horse or cow hair still attached to the leather if nailed on with ½in(13mm) gimp pins, will last longer and the horse hair can be combed and dressed. An advantage of this method is that when the mane wears out it can be taken off and replaced with a new one quite simply.

30. The longest lasting method unfortunately takes the longest time to make. This is a mane using loose horse or cow hair. Two 6in(152mm) by 1in(25mm) wide pieces of thin cotton material (bias binding is very good) are cut out diagonally across the weave of the material. Put a piece of smooth plastic underneath the work as latex glue does not readily stick to plastic. Make sure the hair is clean and free from grease or chemicals, shampoo if necessary. Lay one piece of the material on the plastic and spread a thick layer of glue over it. Lay the ends of the strands of hair in the glue diagonally and along one long side of the material. The last ½in(13mm) at one end should have the hair laid diagonally in the opposite direction, making the forelock. Press the ends of the hair down and put another dribble of glue all along on top of the ends of hair and then press the other cotton strip on top. Put another piece of plastic over the top with a flat weight on and leave to dry. When dry, take the mane out from between the plastic and cut the cloth and glued ends of the hair back to a width of ½in(13mm) (*see* overleaf). With a chisel prepare a slot ½in(13mm) wide and as deep as the mane is thick on the

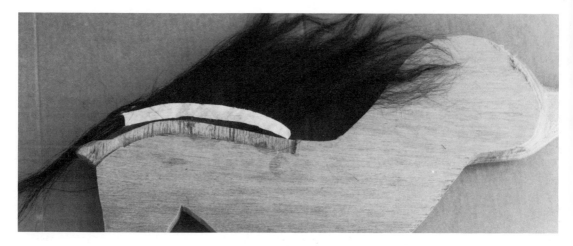

Loose horse hair glued to a cloth strip and ready to glue into the slot chiselled out of the neck of the doll's horse.

inside of one half of the horse stretching from just behind the ear for 6in(152mm) down the edge of the neck so that the two halves of the neck will fit together and hold the mane tightly, but without any force. Try the mane in place first, dry, to check that everything fits correctly and then put latex glue on the outside of both sides of the cotton strip. Smear the insides of the horse with wood glue, put the mane in place (*see* above), clamp the two sides together and leave to dry. Protect the mane from varnish, paint, etc., by holding it between two sheets of plastic held in place with paper clips or by plaiting the hair in such a way that it sticks up away from the body.

> **Tip** If any of the hair of the mane, forelock or tail sticks up and will not smooth down, wrap a damp piece of cloth round the hair and horse to hold the hair in place. Leave to dry slowly.

Tail

31. Drill a hole ¼in(6mm) diameter and ½in(13mm) deep in the centre of the rump and in line with the centre of the back of the neck at a 45°angle to the body (*see* page 35). Sew a piece of fur fabric 2in(51mm) long into a tube, fur side inwards and then turn it fur side out. Put plenty of glue on the open end of the fur fabric and push into the hole with a ½in(13mm) diameter by ⅜in(9mm) long piece of dowel or wood pared down to fit and leave to dry.

32. An alternative method is to cover the ends of suitable lengths of horse or cow hair with glue. Have enough hair so that when bunched together they will just fit the ¼in(6mm) diameter hole. Bind the glue-covered ends together with sewing cotton and push into the tail hole as far as possible and leave to dry.

The patterns for the doll-sized rocking horse are on pages 81 and 82. (Scale 1:3.)

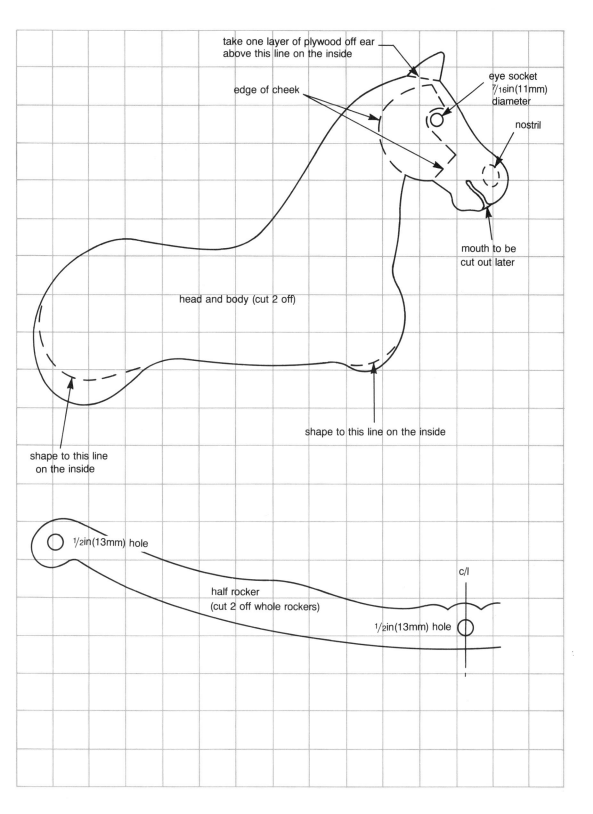

take one layer of plywood off ear
above this line on the inside

eye socket
7/16in(11mm)
diameter

edge of cheek

nostril

head and body (cut 2 off)

mouth to be
cut out later

shape to this line on the inside

shape to this line
on the inside

1/2in(13mm) hole

c/l

half rocker
(cut 2 off whole rockers)

1/2in(13mm) hole

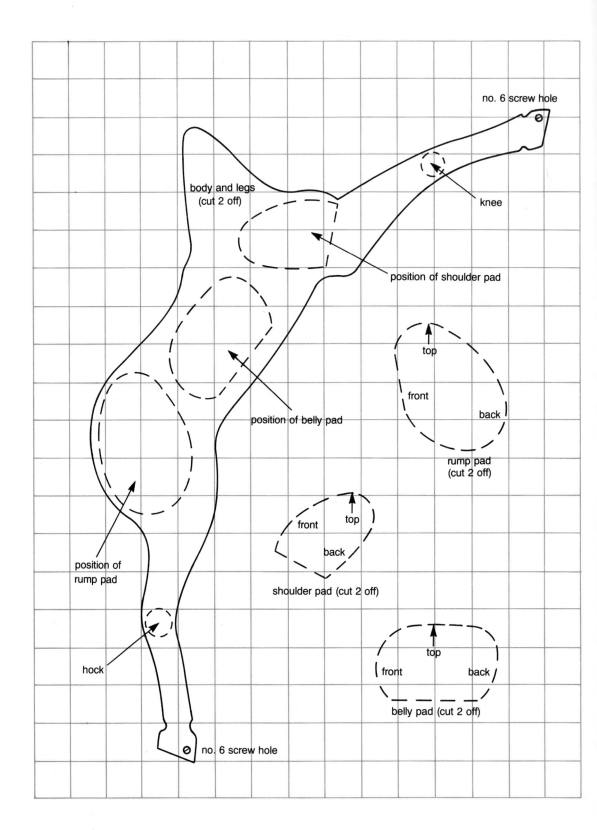

no. 6 screw hole

body and legs
(cut 2 off)

knee

position of shoulder pad

top

front

back

rump pad
(cut 2 off)

position of belly pad

front

top

back

shoulder pad (cut 2 off)

position of
rump pad

top

front

back

hock

belly pad (cut 2 off)

no. 6 screw hole

CHAPTER SEVEN

SMALL, LIGHTLY CARVED HORSE

This is a small horse 22in(560mm) from chest to rump and with a saddle height of 25in(635mm). Strongly made, it is suitable for a child up to the age of five or six years old, depending on how big they grow. The rockers are constructed so that they do not tip at the end of a rock, but slide along the ground instead, both forwards and backwards. The horse can also be put on a swinger stand, details of which are found under 'Swinger Stand' in Chapter 5. Fully tacked up with saddle, stirrups, bridle and reins, the child will feel it has a real rocking horse, but of a size that it will be able to mount without help.

DIMENSIONS

Standing 33in(838mm) high, 25in(635mm) to the saddle on bow rockers of 48in (1,219mm). 13in(330mm) wide across the toes, on a swinger stand 44in(1,118mm) long.

TIME

A minimum of 40 hours, to which drying time must be added.

TOOLS

A band-saw or equivalent. This is a must for cutting out head, rockers and legs

Electric hand drill with sanding attachments including a 5in(125mm) diameter rubber backing disc and a smaller soft backing disc

Sanding discs, one coarse disc, which can be a cintride metal disc for the 5in(125mm) rubber backing disc and one or more fine grit discs for the smaller soft backing attachment

Twist drills, 1 × ¼in(6mm) 1 × ³⁄₁₆in(5mm)

Spade drill, 1 × ¾in(19mm) 1 × ⅞in(22mm)

Chisels, flat bevelled, 1 × 1in(25mm)

1 × ⅜in(9mm)

Gouge 1 × ½in(13mm) No. 8

Mallet

Rifler file, 1 × flat

Saws 1 × cross cut, 1 × tenon

Screwdriver large or medium that will take a No. 8 screw

Tape rule and pencil

Knife for leather

Hammer, chisel peen

Spoke shave, an alternative to the 1in(25mm) flat bevel chisel

Planer or plane

Clamps, 1 × 6in(150mm) and 2 × 8in(200mm) G clamps or equivalent

Tri-square

Note: This horse is a challenge for anyone who has not the time or patience to make a fully carved rocking horse or has done no carving before and is dubious about tackling a fully carved rocking horse. It is carved, so a gouge and two chisels, or the equivalent, are required, but none of the detailed carving of the larger horses is included, such as the carving needed for an open mouth. All the carving work is involved in shaping curves to take the squareness out of the horse, but there is plenty of scope for more carving to be done if so desired.

MATERIALS

Horse

> Head: 1 × softwood 14×8½×2½in
> (355×215×65mm)
> Top plank: 1 × softwood
> 22×7½×2in(560×190×51mm)
> Side plank: 2 × softwood
> 22×3½×2in(560×89×51mm)
> End plank: 2 × softwood
> 3½× 3½×2in(89×89×51mm)
> Bottom plank: 1 × softwood
> 22×3½×2in(560×89×51mm)
> Front leg: 2 × hardwood 1¼(32mm) thick
> (see note)
> Back leg: 2 × hardwood 1¼in(32mm) thick
> (see note)
> Neck overlay: 2 × softwood
> 4½×5½×½in(115×140×13mm)

Note: Overlays for front and back legs are made from the blocks cut out of the corners of the bottom plank. The legs and rockers can be cut from the same piece of hardwood 14×48×1¼in(356×1,220×32mm) *or* the legs and hoof rails if the horse is to be put on a swinger stand can be cut from one piece of hardwood 12×48×1¼in (305×1,220×32mm).

Rockers

> Rockers: 2 × hardwood 1¼in(32mm) thick
> (see note)
> Spacer bars: 2 × hardwood ¾in(19mm)
> diameter 12in(300mm) long

Stand

> Top rail: 1 × softwood
> 40×3×1¼in(1,016×76×32mm)
> Bottom long plank: 1 × softwood
> 44×4¼×1¼in(1,118×108×32mm)
> Bottom cross plank: 2 × softwood
> 16×4×1¼in(406×102×32mm)
> End stop: 2 × softwood
> 4¼×3×1¼in(108×76×32mm)
> Pillar: 2 × hardwood 19×3×3in(483×76×
> 76mm)
> Hoof rail: 2 × hardwood
> 41×2×1¼in(1,041×51×32mm)
> Wedge: 4 × hardwood (see instructions
> following for sizes)
> Swinger bar: 2 × metal ⅜in(9mm)
> diameter rod (see chart)
> Clamp: 2 × metal to suit ⅜in(9mm)
> diameter rod (see chart)
> Cap: 4 × metal to protect swinger bar ends
> Base plate: metal 1/16in(2mm) thick
> ¼in(6mm) to ⅜in(9mm) wide and
> 3in(76mm) to 3½in(88mm) long
> approximately

Note: Details of swinger bar, clamp, cap and base plate are in the chapter on a medium horse (*see* pages 63–4).

CONSTRUCTION

Details are given under five headings for the head as it is much easier to construct in five sections with subheading for other sections before the final assembly.

Accessories

Mane of horsehair 9–10in(225–250mm) base length. The actual hair can be any length, but the suggested length is 12in(300mm). The tail should be ⅝in(16mm) diameter. Again, of any length but the suggested length is 12in(300mm)

Bridle leather strapping ½in(13mm) wide × 40in(1000mm) long

Screw eyelets 2 × metal ½in(13mm)

Stirrups metal 3in(76mm) wide soles

Stirrup straps leather 18in(450mm) long × ⅝in(16mm) wide, adjustable

Reins leather ½in(13mm) wide × 24in (600mm) long

Saddle The saddle cloth would be under 'small' in a catalogue. Otherwise it would be better to take measurements from the actual horse as it depends on what type is required

Nails ½in(13mm) brass domed to nail on all the tack

Suggested amounts are: 20 for the bridle, 12 for the saddle cloth, 24 for the saddle

Head

1. Cut out and plane the head. Draw on the guideline details of the face: draw a line up the centre of the back of the neck, over the ears, down the centre of the forehead and nose, over the mouth and chin, ending up down the centre front of the neck. This line is a guide to help in getting both sides of the head looking equal.

Eyes

2. Drill a ³⁄₁₆in(5mm) diameter hole vertically right through the head at the point where the centre of the eye is marked. This is to make sure that both eyes are level. With a ⅞in(22mm) spade drill, using the ³⁄₁₆in(5mm) diameter hole as central markers, drill ⅜in(9mm) deep to make the sockets for the eyes. The eyes themselves are not set in until the end of construction in order to prevent them from getting damaged.

Nose

3. At ½in(13mm) on either side of the centre line down the nose, make a mark parallel to the centre guideline indicating the nostrils. Put the tenon-saw on this central line and slant it outwards and at 45°. Saw off the three-cornered piece of wood. Do the same with the other nostril. Draw on the sawn surfaces ¾in(19mm) diameter circles which will become the nostrils.

Cheek

4. Carve the rest of the face with the gouge, chisel or spokeshave, whichever you have chosen to use. The large cheek is left flat but the edges are rounded towards the ears, neck and throat. The edge of the cheek, towards the mouth, slants abruptly in from the surface, taking away about ⅛in(3mm) of wood. The area from the straight line of the cheek below the eye to the bridge of the nose and above the nostril is scooped out to leave the bridge of the nose quite narrow and the nostril is standing out by about ⅛in(3mm).

Mouth

5. The mouth area is carved away so that the nostrils stand out all the way round by about ⅛in(3mm). The front of the mouth is then rounded and the wood is slanted back towards the little chin, which is also rounded, as is the wood between the chin and cheek (*see* page 86, top).

Ears

6. On the front of the ear section mark in the two ears. They are ½in(13mm) apart and each is ¾in(19mm) at the base, tapering off from half-way up the ear and rounded at the top. The ears should have no sharp edges or points. With a tenon-saw cut down to the base of the inside edge of each ear. Use a ⅜in(9mm) flat bevel chisel to clear the surplus wood from between the ears. Pare the wood down to the

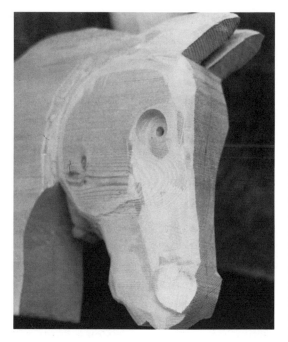

Cut out ears and partly chiselled out face.

Ears and face sanded.

shape of the ears at the sides and round the backs of them. Tidy up between the ears with a rifler file and then hand sand them.

Neck

7.   Cut out, plane, glue and clamp the two neck overlays into position. When dry, the overlays should be chiselled away so that they are still the full thickness at the centre bottom, but slant away to nothing as they get nearer the top of the head. This slanting is carried on to thin down the neck above the overlays and across to the cheek so that the neck is about 1¾in(44mm) thick at the top before widening again for the ears and head. The sides of the overlays are also slanted to nothing and then the chiselling is carried on to round the main wood of the neck at the back and to match the top plank of the body at the front so that when the horse is painted no join of overlays or neck will be visible.

Sanding

8.   Sand the head (*see* below, left) but not the neck, with a coarse sanding disc, changing to a fine disc on a soft backing as soon as most of the chisel marks are removed. Take care not to oversand the nostrils and lose their shape. Hand sand under the chin and the front top of the neck where it cannot be reached with the electric sanding disc.

Mouth

9.   There are two different ways of marking the mouth. Either paint it on over the top coat of paint, before the clear varnish is applied, or indicate where both sides of the mouth are by chiselling a groove ⅛in(3mm) deep as marked on the plans. The front of the mouth has already been cut when the mouth shape was originally sawn. Carefully hand sand the groove.

Body

10.   Cut out the top, bottom, side and end planks of the body. It is important that all pieces are squared and that the corners of

the end planks have precise 90°angles. Plane all the surfaces of the body which need to be glued later, that is, both surfaces of the top and bottom planks and the upper, lower and inner surfaces of the side and end pieces.

11. Glue and clamp the side and end planks to form a hollow oblong box which is 22in(550mm) long by 3½in(88mm) high and 7½in(188mm) wide (see page 46). When the glue is dry replane the top and bottom surfaces of the hollow box to make sure that they are perfectly flat.

12. Mark in the leg slots on the bottom plank of wood as follows: down each side of the upper surface draw a straight line parallel to the long side and 1¾in(44mm) in from it. Draw a pair of similar lines on the under surface parallel to the sides, but 1⅜in(34mm) in from them. On the front and back surfaces join the two sets of lines (this line will be slanting). Measure 3½in(88mm) in from the front edge and mark a line at this distance that runs right round the plank, which will be exactly parallel to the short side of the plank. Draw a similar line 4¾in(122mm) in from the back edge. The four blocks of wood now marked out in the corners are sawn out with the cross-cut saw, which leaves four sockets for the legs to be fitted. Do not discard these blocks of wood.

13. Screw, but do not glue the top plank and bottom plank to the hollow middle box, using four 2½in(63mm) No. 8 screws for each. Draw a line down the centre of the top plank, down the back along the centre of the bottom plank and up the front to meet the line on the top. The body is now ready for shaping.

14. At 2½in(63mm) from the back on the top plank start chiselling the slope that ends in a curve to form the rounded rump. Round the sides of the rump and take away the corners of the hollow middle except for the last ½in(13mm) above where the legs will fit in.

15. Hold the head in place on the body and draw a line round on the top plank so when the carving of the rest of the body is done no wood is removed within that line.

16. From the saddle area of the horse, slope the sides of the top plank down so that there is no uncomfortable ridge where the rider's legs will be. The contours of the sides of the horse are already cut out of the top and bottom planks; chisel out matching areas on the middle, bearing in mind that a horse has very few straight lines, everything is curved (see page 89).

17. With the body upside down on the bench, slope the edges of the V which will be between the back legs, starting wide between the legs and tapering towards the belly and also narrowing until it goes to nothing half-way up the rump and following the contours of the sides of the bottom plank, rounding the edges of the wood to form the belly. Round the edges of the wood between the front legs (see overleaf).

18. The neck of a horse and the top of its shoulders do not continue straight across from his back, but slant downwards towards the muscles at the top of the front legs. Therefore chisel away the wood of the top plank and front top corners of the hollow middle section to within ½in (13mm) of where the top of the legs fit in and bring the line of the neck to a short V at the front.

19. Coarse and then fine sand between where the legs will go on the bottom plank, as this will be hard to do when the whole horse is glued together.

Legs

20. Cut out the two front and two back legs. Plane the top 2in(50mm), both inside and outside of all four legs. To avoid

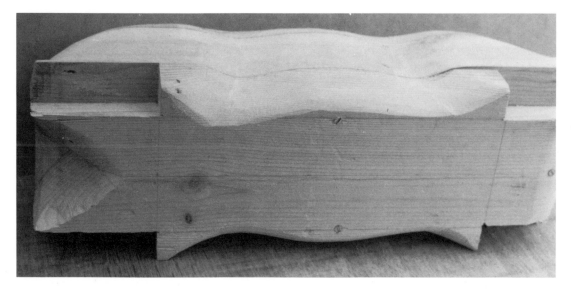

Bottom and side plank details.

confusion mark the outside of each pair of legs.

21. Draw a line ¼in(6mm) down and parallel to the outside top of each leg. Lay the top of the leg on the slanting bed (102.5) of the band-saw or equivalent, and saw through the top of each leg along the line marked. This will give the top of each leg a slant so that it will fit snugly into the sockets made in the corners of the bottom plank.

22. Using a chisel, round off the edges of the legs to within 2in(51mm) of the top except for the knees and hocks which are left rather angular as they are naturally. Make a groove just above and below the point of the hocks both inside and out.

23. Coarse sand the whole of the legs except the top 2in(51mm) including rounding the edges of the knees, hocks and hooves. Finish with a fine soft sanding ready for painting.

24. Drill two ³⁄₁₆in(5mm) diameter holes within the top 2in(51mm) of each leg. Glue and screw with 2in(51mm) No. 8 screw.

the four legs into the sockets made in the bottom plank. When dry, take out the screws, drill the screw holes bigger and put in ⅜in(9mm) dowels. Cut off any surplus dowel and leave to dry.

Rockers

25. Cut out the two and plane the sides. Clamp them together and sand the tops and bottoms with a coarse and then a fine sanding paper so that the two rockers become a perfect match. This is important, especially on the undersides, as mismatching will cause uneven rocking and may make a timid rider feel unstable.

26. Drill two ³⁄₁₆in(5mm) diameter holes right through both rockers where indicated on the plans and countersink the four outside tops of the holes that are showing in the sides of the rockers. Unclamp the rockers and on the inside, using the four holes as centre guides, drill ¼in(6mm) deep with the spade drill. Measure from half-way across the tip of the front hoof to the corresponding place on the other front hoof. Likewise with the

back two hooves. These two measurements are the size of the whole of the width of the rockers when completed. To get the length of ³⁄₄in(19mm) diameter dowel to be cut for the two spacer bars, using the two measurements of the hoof tips, take away the width of the rocker times two and add on ½in(13mm) which allows for the drilled recess. Separately measure each pair of hoof tips to cut the spacer bars as very often the distance between the hoof tips are not the same. Glue and screw the spacer bars into their positions on the insides of the rockers with 1¼in(32mm) No. 8 countersunk screws. Check with a square that the rockers are not crooked or twisted, cover the screw

heads with wood filler and leave to dry. Sand the top and bottom edges smooth.

27. Plane the underside of the neck of the horse. Drill four ³⁄₁₆in(5mm) diameter holes within the area that the head will cover on the top plank. Glue the underside of the neck and screw it into position, putting the screws through from the underside of the top plank. When dry replace the screws with ³⁄₈in(9mm) dowels.

28. Screw the body of the horse together again and set it on the rockers, putting it far enough forward so that the head is not dipping down. With a ⁷⁄₈in(22mm) straight edge mark and cut out the rebates in the hooves (*see* page 52). Drill a

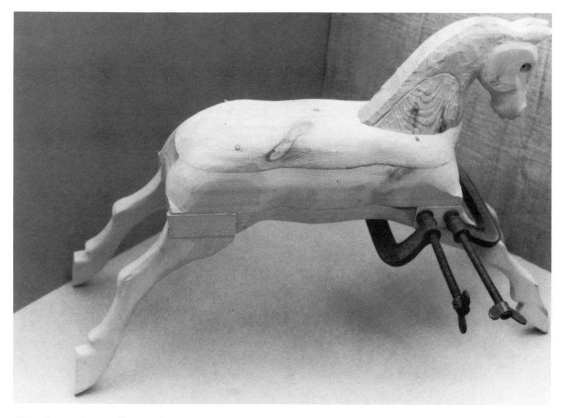

Clamping on the top of leg overlay.

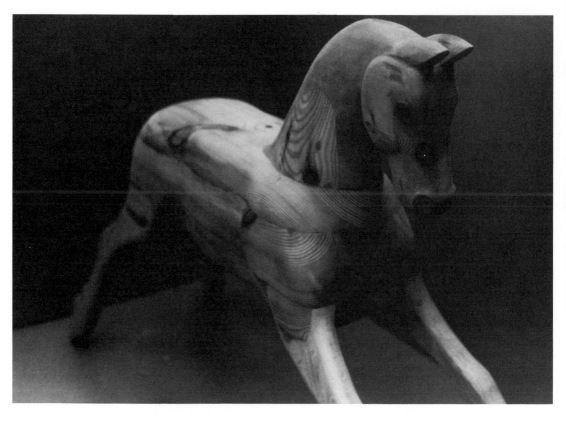

Completed horse sanded and ready for painting.

¼in(6mm) diameter hole through each hoof and through the rocker it is standing on. Take it off.

29. Glue and screw the three parts of the body together and when dry replace the screws with ⅜in(9mm) dowels.

30. To make the overlays for the tops of the legs, use the four blocks of wood that were cut from the corners of the bottom plank to make the leg sockets. Plane the sawn slanting side and then lay them on the top of the legs with the slanting side inwards. Mark a line along the top of each block level with the body and cut off with the band-saw any excess wood beyond that line. Glue and clamp into position (*see* page 89). When dry, chisel each overlay so that it tapers to nothing down the leg and is rounded at the side to match the rest of the wood.

31. Coarse sand the body and neck.

32. Inspect the whole horse and fill in any blemishes with wood filler. Soft sand the horse and then finally hand sand with medium sanding paper (*see* above).

Eyes

33. The eyes can now be put in. Fill the eye socket with wood filler, press the eye into the socket while the filler is still soft and wipe away any excess wood filler that oozes out from round the eye. Hand sand any roughness left by the wood filler.

The rocking horse is now complete. *See* page 65 for the painting. For dressing *see* Chapter 4. Finally the horse is bolted by its hooves to the rockers with M6 roofing bolts, length as required.

The patterns for the small, lightly carved rocking horse are on pages 91–4. (Scale 1:3.)

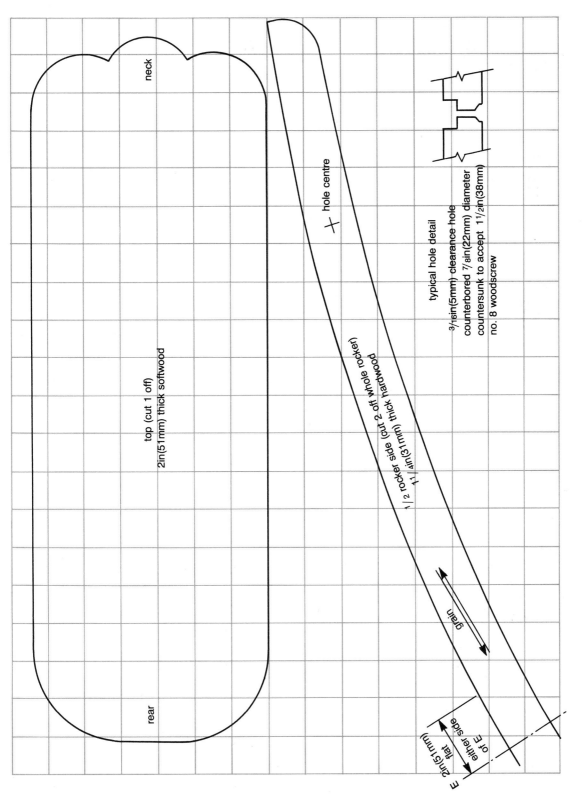

neck

top (cut 1 off)
2in(51mm) thick softwood

rear

hole centre

1/2 rocker side (cut 2 off whole rocker)
1¹/₄in(31mm) thick hardwood

grain

E 2in(51mm)
flat
either side
of E

typical hole detail

³/₁₆in(5mm) clearance hole
counterbored ⁷/₈in(22mm) diameter
countersunk to accept 1¹/₂in(38mm)
no. 8 woodscrew

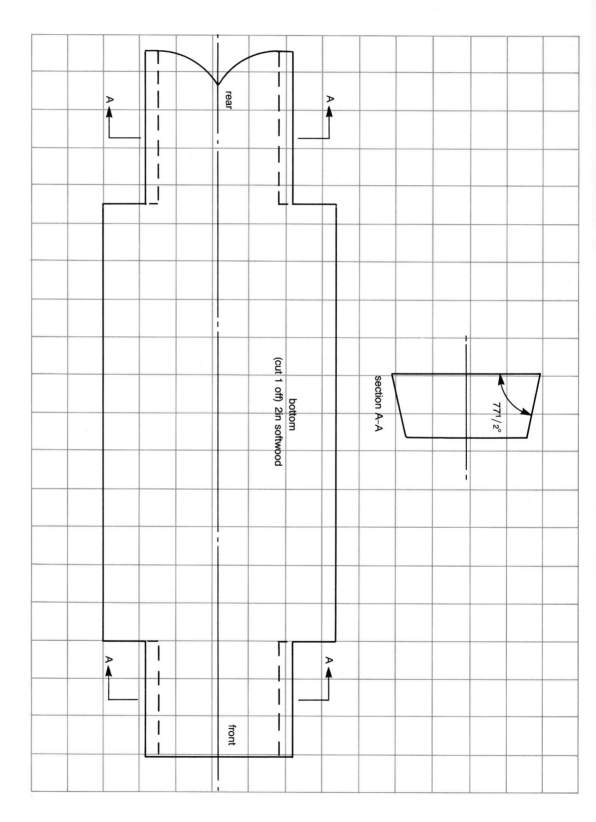

rear

bottom
(cut 1 off) 2in softwood

front

section A-A

77$^1/_2$°

A   A

A   A

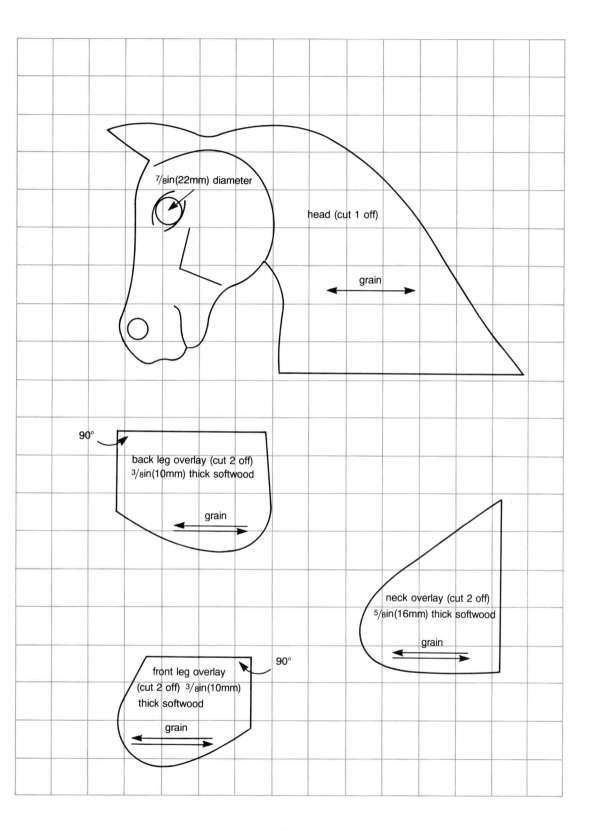

7/8in(22mm) diameter

head (cut 1 off)

grain

90°

back leg overlay (cut 2 off)
3/8in(10mm) thick softwood

grain

neck overlay (cut 2 off)
5/8in(16mm) thick softwood

grain

front leg overlay
(cut 2 off) 3/8in(10mm)
thick softwood

grain

90°

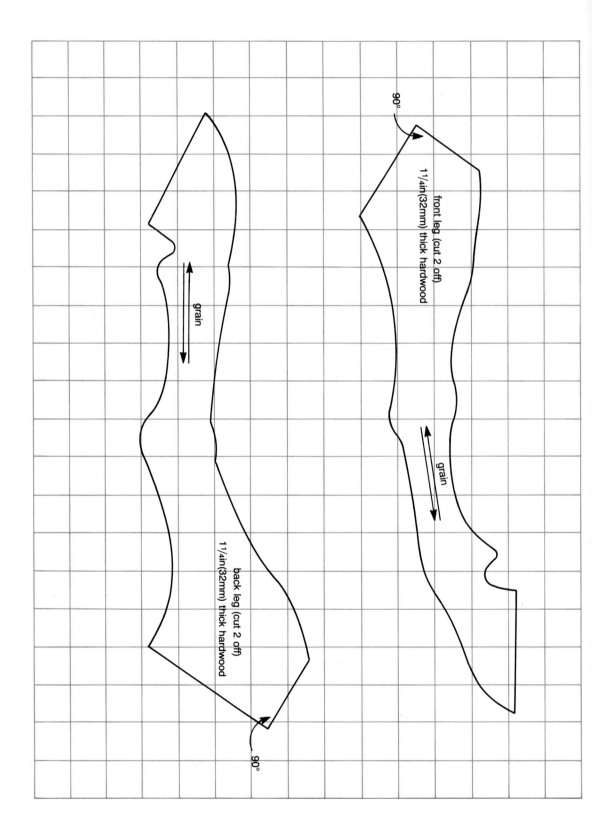

front leg (cut 2 off)
1¹/₄in (32mm) thick hardwood

90°

grain

back leg (cut 2 off)
1¹/₄in (32mm) thick hardwood

90°

grain

CHAPTER EIGHT

TODDLERS' HORSES

Unlike any of the other rocking horses that are covered in this book, these two sizes of toddlers' horses have no carving, which makes them just right for a beginner. It could be given as a present to a small child by someone intending to make a fully carved larger horse later on, so that the child will be used to the idea of a rocking horse, while giving the maker time to make one to a more elaborate design. They are ideal for pre-school groups where the children using them never get any older.

Toddlers enjoy their horse so much that it is very rarely out of use, so it must be constructed sturdily, which is the case with this design. It is also very easily and quickly made with the minimum number of tools. The design allows them to slide instead of tipping at the end of each rock. The horses can be made with any thickness of plywood from 5/8in(16mm) upwards. Obviously if a very thick plywood is used, they will look out of proportion. There is the advantage that they can be made out of oddments of plywood, provided they are all of good quality. Shuttering plywood should not be used. The sizes of the oddments must be large enough to take the whole of one part of the plan on each piece. The thickness can be built up so that all the parts are the same thickness by gluing together these pieces, thereby making a lovely toy out of offcuts at a really quite minimal cost. Alternatively it can be made out of just one large piece of plywood and two other pieces of wood.

The smaller horse would suit a toddler from about one-and-a-half years old, or when they are quite steady on their feet, and would probably last about two or more years. The larger horse is meant for a slightly older child and they would outgrow it when they reach about five years of age.

TIME

It requires approximately 10 hours to make plus the time needed for the paint to dry. There are two sizes of toddler rocking horse plans. The first set of details are for the smaller horse.

DIMENSIONS

Standing 21in(533mm) high, 12in(305mm) to the seat, 31in(787mm) long including the rockers, 11½in(292mm) across at the widest point which is the footrest.

TOOLS (ONE OF EACH)

Band-saw or equivalent such as a fretsaw
Tenon-saw
Medium screwdriver that will slot into No. 6 screws
Tape rule, pencil
Brace or
Electric hand drill and 5in(127mm) rubber-backed sanding attachment
5in(127mm) coarse and medium sanding discs
$\frac{3}{4}$in(19mm) spade drill to drill hole for handles
$\frac{3}{16}$in(5mm) twist drill to drill holes for No. 8 screws
$\frac{1}{8}$in(3mm) twist drill to drill pilot holes in the backrest
$\frac{1}{2}$in(13mm) twist drill only for the alternative way of securing a fabric tail
2 × 3in(76mm) clamps
Vice or substitute
One sheet of 60 grit sanding paper
Some $\frac{3}{4}$in(19mm) wide approximately, paint brushes. The number will depend on how many colours and types of paint are used
One fine paint brush to paint the face details
Needle and cotton if the fur fabric is used

Tip If the rocking horse is to have a plain wood finish when completed, before cutting out check that the plywood to be used is the same colour and type of wood on both sides. If the two sides are different, to get a horse that has the same colour and type of wood on the legs, front and back of the same side, turn the pattern over for one of each pair. That will give each pair of legs matching plywood on the outside surfaces.

MATERIALS

1 × 36×24×$\frac{5}{8}$in(914×610×16mm) good quality facing plywood out of which four legs, one head, two neck muscles, one seat, two backrests, two rockers, one footrest and one spacer bar will be cut
1 × 13$\frac{1}{2}$×3$\frac{1}{2}$×2in(343×89×51mm) softwood block for the body
1 × 6in(152mm) long by $\frac{3}{4}$in(19mm) diameter wood dowel or similar piece of wood to be used as handles
4 × 1×$\frac{1}{2}$in(25×13mm) metal brackets with two screw holes in each. The size must not exceed 1$\frac{1}{4}$in(31mm) long
18 × 1in(25mm) No. 8 countersink screws
8 × $\frac{1}{2}$in(13mm) No. 6 countersink screws. No larger
2 × 2in(51mm) No. 8 countersink screws
2 × 3×$\frac{1}{4}$in(75×6mm) dowel to secure head to body
1 × 12×4in(304×102mm) piece of fur fabric from which to make the mane and tail. This is optional
4 × $\frac{1}{2}$in(13mm) gimp pins to use with the fur fabric
Small quantities of latex to glue the mane on, epoxy resin to glue the horse together and wood filler
Small cans of paint depending on the finish required, such as sealer and clear varnish for a plain wood finish or primer, undercoat and top coat for the painted version. A small can of aerosol black paint (the same type of paint as the top coat) to do the dappling
20 × small $\frac{1}{2}$in(13mm) circular sticky-backed paper discs for the dappling effect

CONSTRUCTION

1. Cut out all the pieces of the horse and rockers from the plans.
2. Mark and drill all the positions of the screws with a $\frac{3}{16}$in(5mm) drill, except the two positions on the backrests.
3. Cut a hole in the head where marked

Back row (left to right): Large horse on rockers, large horse on swinger stand, medium horse on swinger stand, medium horse on rockers. Front row: Small horse on rockers, toddler's horse, doll-sized horse, tiny horse.

Large, medium and small rocking horses on rockers.

Large and medium rocking horses on swinger stands, dappled with an air brush.

Doll's and toddler's rocking horses. Neither of these need carving with chisels.
Toddler's horse with dappling is done with spray paint over removable paper circles.

An 1820 rocking horse head. This and the following two heads from 1840 and 1860
show the very individual styles of the prefactory-made horses.

An 1840 rocking horse head.

The effects of dappling done with a sponge dipped in black paint.

An old Ayres horse ready for a refit. A good example of the patchy dappling used by both Triang and Lines Ltd and copied by many other makers.

Piebald small horse with simple rockers and saddle. All nailed-on tack.

Giving comparative sizes of the small, small toddler's and doll-sized horses.

The tiny carved horse, real horsehair mane and tail, leather tack and felt saddle cloth.

The larger toddler's rocking horse with a painted mane and fur fabric tail.

An 1860 rocking horse head.

The head of a restored old horse, originally sold by Selfridge Store, London. Note the painting round the eye and the brass rosette.

A restored rocking horse from the last quarter of the nineteenth century. Note the deep boat-shaped rockers. The dappling is done with a stippling brush on a blue/grey background.

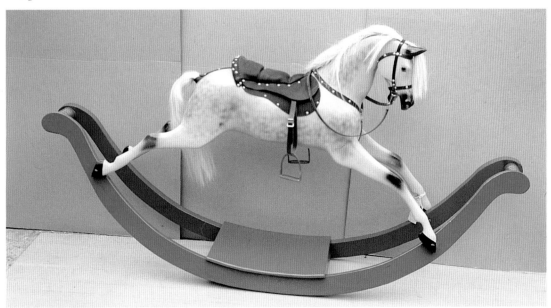

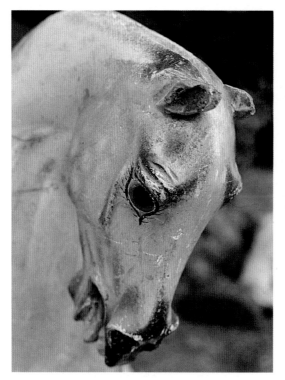

The beautifully carved face of an early Ayes horse. This is one of the first horses to have a swinger stand.

A completely restored old horse.

The more unusual early Triang rocking horse, now fully restored.

with a ¾in(19mm) spade drill, the exact diameter of the dowling (or similar) to be used for the handles, as they will only be glued holding it in position. Any slack and the rider will soon work it loose and spoil the toy.

4. Glue and clamp the backrest pieces on top of each other and when dry, sand round all the edges and sides except the bottom. Drill approximately ¼in(6mm) with a ³⁄₁₆in(5mm) drill down through the marks for the two screws that go into the backrest. Complete the screw holes with a ⅛in(3mm) pilot hole drill.

Body

5. The block of wood is the main body of the horse. Draw two lines ½in(13mm) from each top side along the body. On each end of the body where the lines finish at the top edge, draw a line from that point to the two outer corners. Saw off the triangles of wood so formed and discard. Plane smooth the two sawn-off surfaces and the top and bottom surfaces.

Tail

6. If a fur fabric tail is to be fitted: cut a 3in(75mm) long by 6½in(165mm) wide strip of fur fabric. Fold it longways with the fur side innermost. Note at this point which way the fur is lying so that the tail will have the fur pointing downwards. Sew the cut long sides together and the end where the fur is pointing downwards. Turn the tail right side out. The end to be glued is the unsewn end.

7. One way to fit the tail into the horse is to make 1in(25mm) long by ¾in(19mm) wide by ¼in(6mm) deep groove on top at the centre back of the body. Smear the groove with glue and nail the tail into the groove with four gimp pins. This way the tail is very secure but needs protection when the horse is being painted, e.g. as a small bag held in place with rubber bands.

8. The alternative way is to drill a ½in(13mm) diameter 1in(25mm) deep hole in the back of the body part of the horse, cover the end of the tail with glue and push it as far as possible into the hole. All this can be done after the last coat of paint is dry, but the tail is not quite so secure and will, with plenty of energetic waggling by a toddler, come loose in time.

9. Glue and screw the top of the body down the centre of the length of the underside of the seat with four 1in(25mm) No. 8 screws through the screw holes in the seat. Make sure that all screws, except those used on the metal brackets, are countersunk below the surface of the wood so that they can be covered with wood filler and there will be no danger of the toddler getting scratched.

Head

10. Saw a slot the length indicated on the seat plan and the exact width of the plywood head (*see* below), through both the

The mortice cut ready to receive the head tenon.

seat and the body. Try dry first, and when it is a good fit, smear the tenon of the head section with glue and slide it into the slot. Check that the bottom edge of the head behind the tenon is touching the seat along all its length.

11.   Drill two holes to take the ¼in(6mm) dowels, right through the front sides of the body to secure the head in its position. These two dowel holes should be so placed that they do not interfere with the screws that will be used to hold the front legs in place (*see* below). Cover the dowels with glue and tap in position. Saw off any surplus.

Backrest

12.   Glue and screw with two 2in(51mm) screws the backrest to the seat so that the back is flush with the back edge of the seat.

Legs

13.   Chamfer approximately ⅛in(3mm) off the top of all four legs so that the slope formed will make the legs fit snugly underneath the seat and against the body of the horse. As the legs are very similar in shape, except that the hooves are pointing in opposite directions, be careful to make sure that the front legs are at the front and back legs underneath the seat and backrest.

14.   Glue and screw with two 1in(25mm) screws, each of the four legs into position. Sand away any unevenness at the front and back of the horse.

15.   Fill in with wood filler any gaps left by splinters and sand smooth all edges of the horse and rockers, except the inside of the hooves.

The cross shows the position of a leg screw which misses the dowels being put in to hold the head tenon.

Rockers

16. Make a pencil mark 5in(127mm) from the front ends of the two rockers. These are the positions of the front hoof tips of the horse. Glue and screw the front hooves to the rockers with one 1in(25mm) screw each. The rockers are on the inside of the hooves and it is necessary for there to be a clearance of ⅛in(3mm) between the hoof tips and the bottom edge of the rockers. Glue and screw the back two hooves on the rockers as well.

Footrest and Spacer

17. Turn the horse upside-down and clamp it in the vice (or substitute). Make a pencil mark 8in(203mm) from the front on the inside of each rocker. Hold the footrest underneath the rockers with the front edge in line with the pencil marks and overlapping the sides of the rockers. Put one of the metal brackets in position where it will eventually be screwed to the underside of the footrest and the side of the rocker. It will be noted that the angle of the bracket

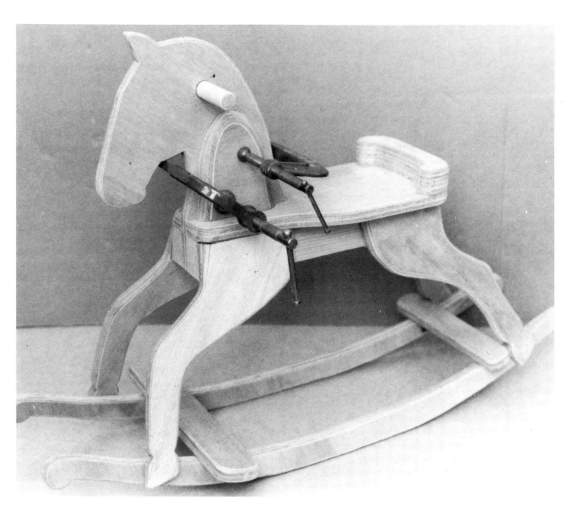

Neck overlays being clamped on before the rocking horse is painted.

The top brackets as bought. The bottoms bracket bent out and screwed into position.

is not wide enough. Bend the bracket to fit (102½°) and bend the other three brackets to match (*see* above). Once more line up the footrest, making sure that it is overlapping by the same amount each side of the rockers, 2½in(64mm) approximately. Place two of the brackets in position against the rockers and also central on the underside of the footrest. Screw with two ½in(13mm) No. 6 screws. The screws should be no longer or they may poke through the footrest; if they do, file them flush with the footrest.

18. Make a pencil mark 7in(178mm) from the back on the inside of each rocker. Put the back spacer underneath the rockers and line up the back edge against the pencil marks so that the overlap of the rockers is the same each side. Screw the two remaining brackets to the sides of the rockers and to the underside of the back spacer, as for the footrest. Ensure that both sides of the footrest and spacer bar are resting on the rockers as well as the brackets and not the brackets alone. The rocking horse is now rigid as the footrest and spacer bar give it extra strength and make the rockers and legs stable.

Handles

19. Round off the edges of the large dowel (or similar) which is to be used for the handles. Smear the centre with glue and push through the hole in the head so that it protrudes the same distance on either side and leave to dry.

Neck Muscles

20. Sand all the outside edges except the bottom edge of the neck muscles and glue on in the place shown in the plans. Making sure the bottom edges are in contact with the seat. Use two clamps to secure them in position and leave the horse to dry (*see* page 99).

21. Cover all screw heads with wood filler and sand smooth.

Painting

22. If a fur fabric mane is to be used, keep clear of all paint an area 8in(203mm) from the back of the ears down the edge of the head and neck and 1½in(38mm) down the forelock, where the mane and forelock are glued on. Seal the rest of the horse and rockers with two coats of sealer, rubbing down any roughness with sanding paper after each seal.

23. If it is stay a plain wood colour, put on at least two coats of clear varnish. Polyurethane is very good as it is a very hard gloss finish and will withstand any minor knocks or scrapes.

24. For the painted version, paint with

successive coats, one primer, one under-coat and one gloss top coat. One or any number of colours can be used for the top finishing coat depending on preference. For the dappling effect, *see* page 69 and 'Painting' on page 68 in Chapter 5 on the medium horse.

Mane

25. Using the fur fabric, cut one strip 8in(203mm) long and ⅞in(22mm) wide. Glue the strip with latex glue to the bare patch on the head and neck to make the mane. Do the same with a 1½in(38mm) long by ⅞in(22mm) wide strip and glue it onto the forehead which will make the forelock. Sheepskin can be used instead of fur fabric.

26. The alternative is to paint on the mane and forelock with a contrasting colour.

Face

27. The ½in(13mm) diameter eyes are painted with a fine brush in black gloss paint, one third or 33 per cent of the way down the head measuring from the bottom of the ears (*see* page 78). If two white dots are painted to one side of the centre of the pupil, the eye will look more alive. Do not paint a dot in the centre of the pupil because this will have the effect of making the horse blind.

28. A fraction of a curl towards the bridge of the nose given to the end of the line for the mouth, which is 1¼in(32mm) long, gives a happy look to the face. A curl towards the chin has the opposite effect; the horse looks miserable. Horses have no noticeable eyebrows.

29. The curls to represent the nostrils are not quite at the end of the nose, there must be room for the top lip. If at all unsure of where to put the details of the face, mark them in first with something that can be wiped off and then check that they are reasonably even with the other side.

30. A further detail that can be added, is to paint a bridle on the face. Paint ¼in(6mm) wide lines, use the photographs of bridles in this book to show where the bridle should be painted.

The patterns for the small toddler's rocking horse are on pages 102–4. (Scale 1:2.)

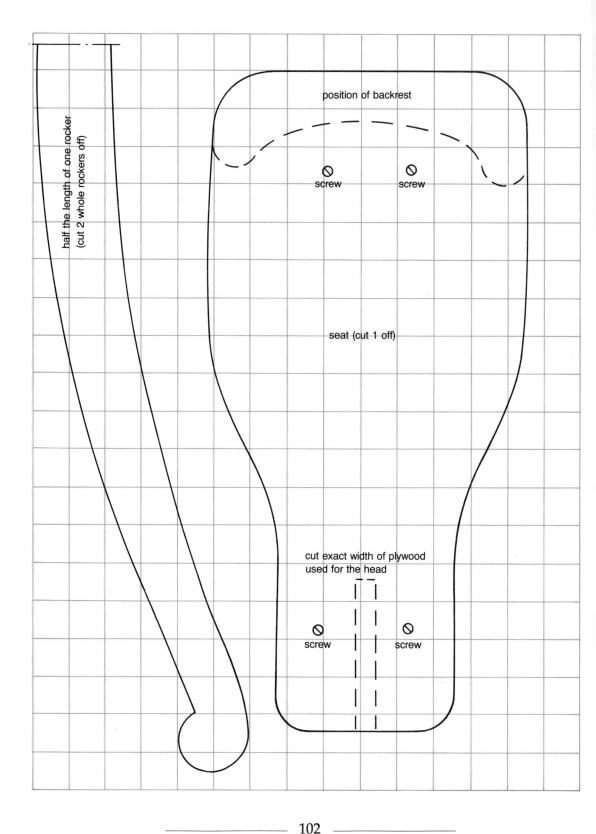

half the length of one rocker
(cut 2 whole rockers off)

position of backrest

⊘
screw

⊘
screw

seat (cut 1 off)

cut exact width of plywood
used for the head

⊘
screw

⊘
screw

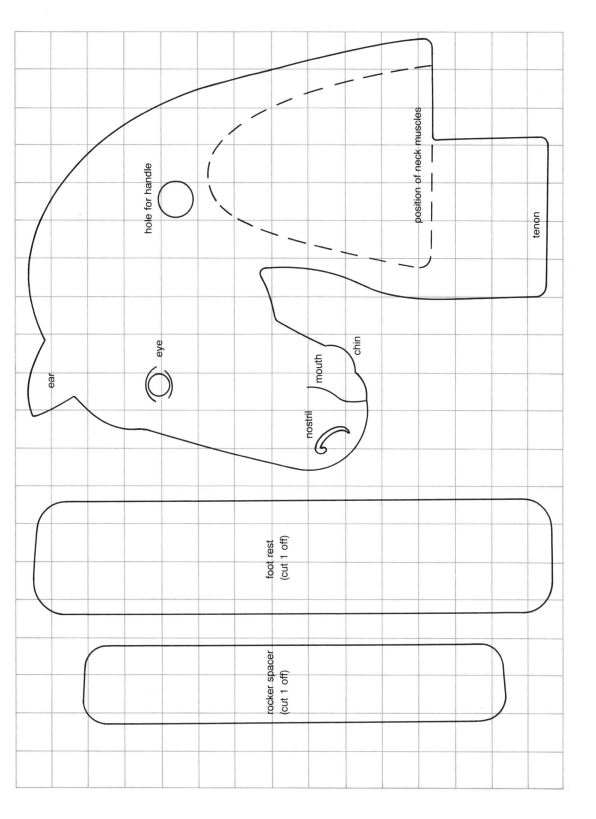

hole for handle

position of neck muscles

tenon

ear

eye

nostril

mouth

chin

foot rest
(cut 1 off)

rocker spacer
(cut 1 off)

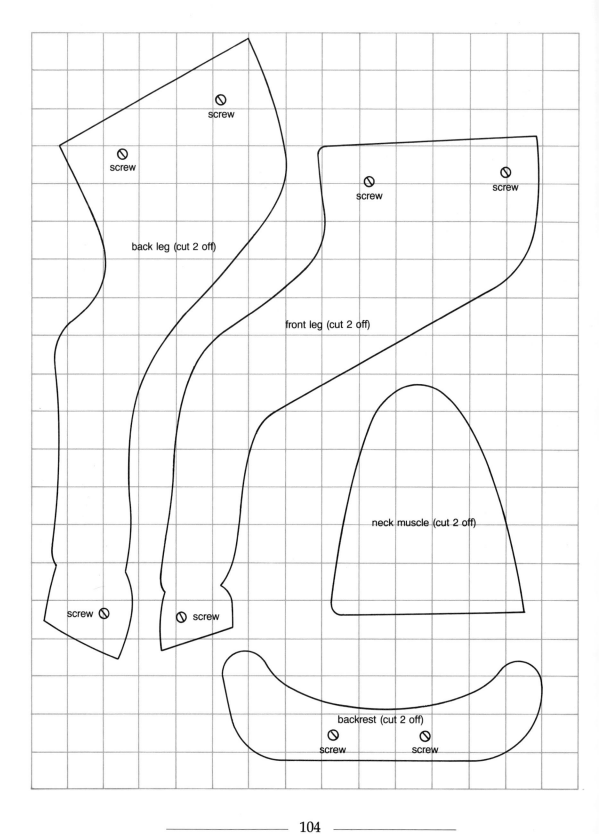

THE LARGER TODDLER'S ROCKING HORSE

This is no more difficult to make than the smaller one, just larger sizes on some things for a toddler with longer legs.

Dimensions

Standing 25in(635mm) high, 14in(356mm) to the seat, 33in(838mm) long including the rockers, 12¾in(324mm) across by the foot-rest.

Time

Ten hours plus time for paint and glue to dry.

Materials

> 1 × 48×24×¾in(1,219×610×19mm) facing plywood
> 1 × 14½×3½×2in(368×89×51mm) softwood block for the body
> 14 × 4in(356×102mm) piece of fur fabric for mane and tail, optional

All other materials are the same as for the small toddler's horse.

Tools

All tools are the same as for the small toddler's rocking horse.

Construction

Follow the same construction details except for two of the measurements – the footrest overlaps the rockers by 2⅜in (60mm) each side and there is 7in(178mm) between the ends of the rockers and back spacer bar.

The minimum width of plywood must be ¾in(19mm) to make sure that the longer legs on this horse are just as sturdy as the smaller toddler's rocking horse.

Both these toddlers' rocking horses should, with normal use, outlast the length of time a rider is small enough to use them. They should give hours of pleasure to their small rider and his or her friends.

The patterns for the larger toddler's rocking horse appear on pages 106–9. (Scale 1:2.)

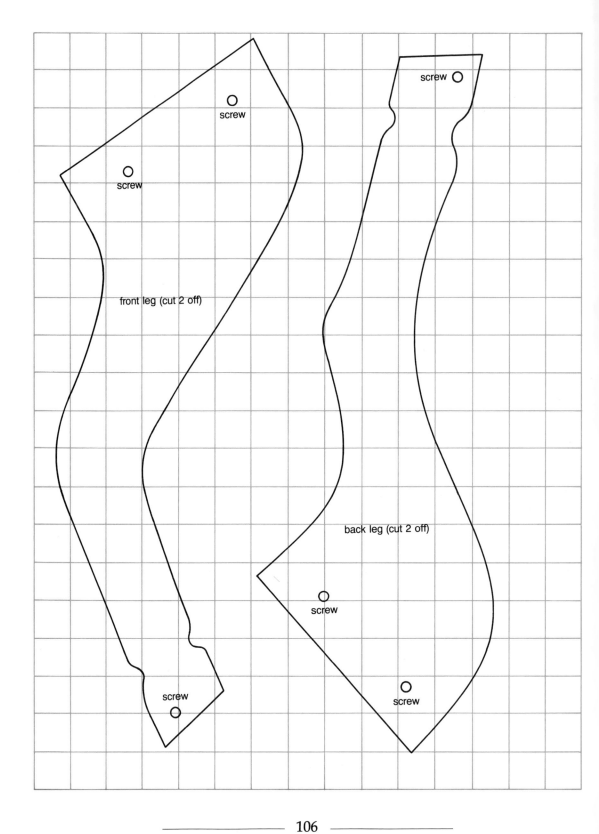

front leg (cut 2 off)

back leg (cut 2 off)

screw

screw

screw

screw

screw

screw

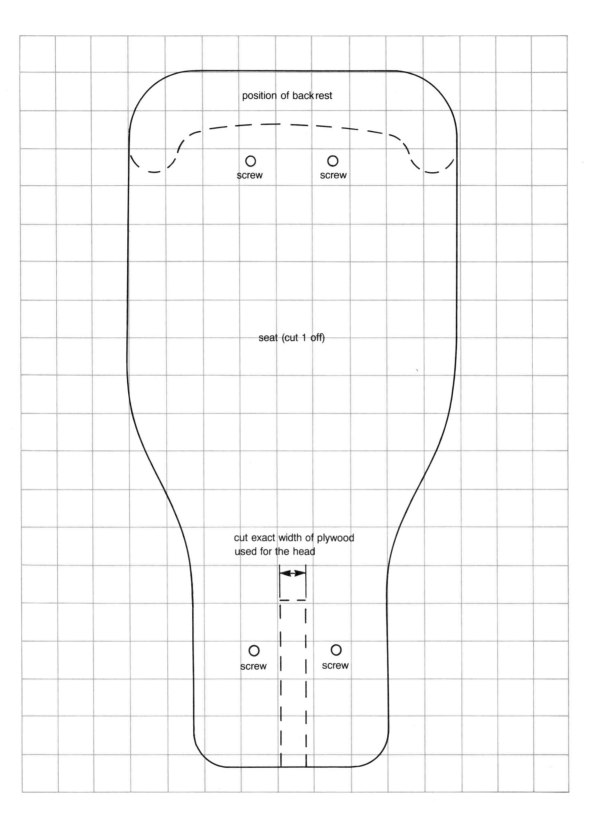

position of backrest

screw   screw

seat (cut 1 off)

cut exact width of plywood
used for the head

screw   screw

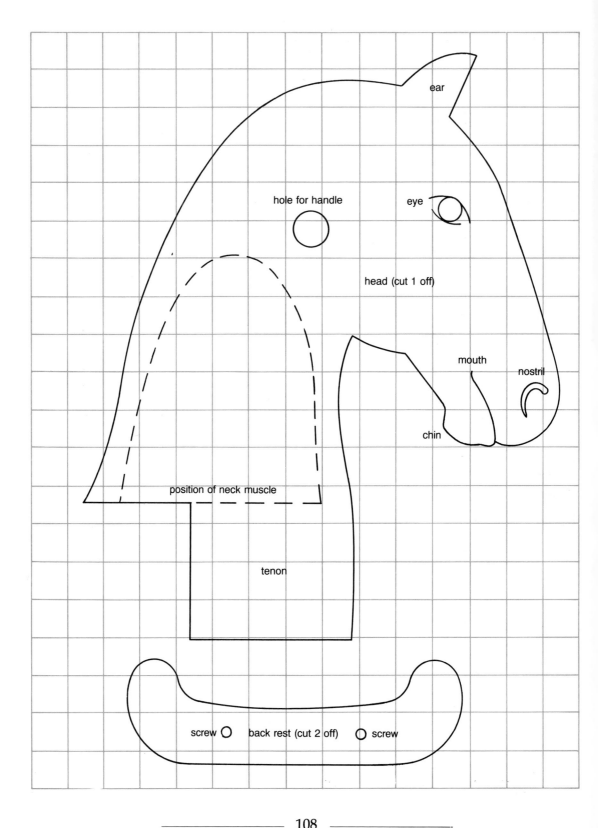

ear

hole for handle

eye

head (cut 1 off)

mouth

nostril

chin

position of neck muscle

tenon

screw ○   back rest (cut 2 off)   ○ screw

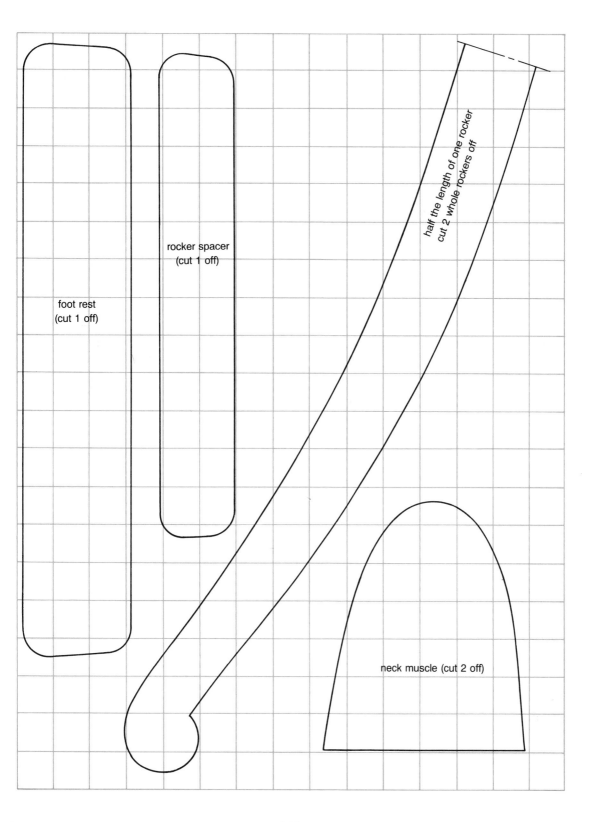

foot rest
(cut 1 off)

rocker spacer
(cut 1 off)

half the length of one rocker
cut 2 whole rockers off

neck muscle (cut 2 off)

CHAPTER NINE

LARGE ROCKING HORSE ON SWINGER STAND AND ROCKER

LARGE HORSE ON SWINGER STAND

This is a very majestic rocking horse, tall, with its neck arched and showing strength in the well-formed muscles of the body and legs. It can also have fine details such as a tongue and palate in the mouth. Providing there is room, for it would need a minimum of 9ft(3m) length in order to allow it to swing freely, this is the horse for a family with a wide range of ages. It is large enough for a small adult to ride within reason, but a heavy teenage boy trying to win the Derby would do it no good. Yet it is gentle enough in movement to be enjoyed by a young child (under supervision), and it has a back which is quite long enough to allow two small riders to have lots of fun riding together.

The gait of this horse is not suitable for use with rockers, therefore only details of a swinger stand are given.

Dimensions

Standing 50in(1,270mm) high, 38in (965mm) to the top of the saddle, 29in(737mm) from breast to rump, grading it a large horse and standing on a 60in(156mm) long swinger stand.

Time

It takes a minimum of sixty hours to make, to which drying time for the glue and paint must be added.

Tools

The requirements are the same as for the medium horse except that the minimum length for the sash clamps is 12in(305mm) and spade drill for the eye sockets is 1½in(38mm) diameter.

Materials

The head is tall so the main head (without overlays) can be made from two pieces of wood glued together before the head is cut out. The join can be seen on the forehead of the horse on page 41 (top). Have the join at the top of the head and securely do-welled, never at the bottom of the neck which would also include the nose.

Note: If narrow planks are to be used, glue two pieces together to make the larger overlays. The front and back legs can be cut out of the same 51×20×1½in (1,295×508×38mm) plank as the hoof rails.

All parts of the stand are made of softwood except the pillars and hoof rail. *See* diagrams and charts for sizes (pages 60–4).

Head: 1 × softwood 19×12½×3in(483×318× 76mm)

Top plank: 1 × softwood 29×9×2in(737× 229× 51mm)

Side plank: 2 × softwood 29×5×2in(737× 127×51mm)

End plank: 2 × softwood 5×5×3in(127× 127×76mm)

Front legs: 2 × hardwood 1½in(38mm) thick (see note)

Back legs: 2 x 1½in(38mm) thick (*see* note)

Eyes glass: 2 × brown iris 1⅛in(28mm) diameter

Given below are the sizes of the pieces of wood that are needed if every overlay is to be cut individually.

Overlays: measurements are all length × width × thickness

Ears: 2 × 4½×1½×¼in(114×38×6mm)

Cheek/face: 2 × 6×6×⅜in(152×152×9mm)

Large neck: 2 × 9×10×1in(229×250×25mm)

Small neck: 2 × 4¾×7×1in(121×178×25mm)

Shoulder: 2 × 10×5×½in(250×127×13mm)

Ribs: 2 × 9×5×½in(229×127×13mm)

Top rump: 1 × 6½×8×¾in (165×203×19mm)

Side rump: 2 × 8×4¾×½in (203×121× 13mm)

Inside leg front: 2 × 3½×4¾×¾in (89×121×19mm)

Inside leg back: 2 × 4¼×5¼×¾in (108×133×19mm)

Corner of leg: 4 × 2½×2×¾in (64×51×19mm)

Outside leg front: 2 x 5½×6¾×1¼in (140×171× 32mm)

Outside leg back: 2 × 6½×6×1¼in (165×152×32mm)

Hooves: 8 × 3½×3×½in(89×76×13mm)

Top rail: 1 ×

Bottom long plank: 1 ×

Bottom cross plank: 2 ×

End stop: 2 ×

Hoof rail: 2 × hardwood

Pillars: 2 × hardwood

Swinger bars: 2 × metal

Clamp: 2 × metal to take ½in(13mm) bar

Base plate: 2 × metal 3 to 3½in(76 to 89mm) long by ½ to ⅝in(13 to 16mm) wide and 1⁄16in(2mm) thick

Roofing bolts: 2 × M6 × 2in(51mm), 4 × M6 length as required

Screws countersink: 4 × 1¼in(32mm) No. 8, 12 x 2½in(64mm) No. 8

Gimp pins: 4 × ½in(13mm)

Split pins: 4 × 1⁄16in(2mm) diameter

End caps: 4 × metal 1⅝in(41mm) diameter ½in(13mm) deep

Nails: 12 × ½in(13mm)

Accessories

Mane and tail, bridle, bit, reins, saddle, stirrup-straps, stirrups, saddle cloth, martingale and cropper strap. All the options are open for this size of horse, so refer to the chapter on accessories before deciding on type and colour. For instance, if making a horse that is suitable for older children as well as the young ones, it is ideal to put on a removable bridle, saddle and martingale. A decision on this needs to be made before carving commences because if everything is going to be removable the body has to be drilled or carved to fit the saddle, depending on which type of removable saddle is to be used.

Space in the workshop is needed to make this horse as in the final stages there must be enough room to swing the horse round to sand and paint it. It is heavy too, despite its hollow middle, especially when it is complete and on its stand. It certainly is not a rocking horse that you want to constantly move around.

Construction and Carving

There is not a great deal of difference between actually making a large horse and a medium one. You can therefore follow the instructions for the medium horse alongside the details below, superimposing the larger sizes. The instructions for this horse are the same as those for the medium horse in Chapter 5. However, where a numbered instruction is given below, replace the corresponding instruction from the relevant section in Chapter 5 with the one given here as there is a variation in construction.

The most conspicuous difference between the horses is that the large horse has overlays put on instead of making the wood thicker. This cuts down on cost, weight and time during construction, as a good proportion of the extra wood would be carved away. The overlays have been made larger than needed so that when the carving is being done there will be no edge to interrupt in the forming of the muscles and curves. The edges and thickness of the overlays can be carved and sanded away to whatever extent the maker requires. The depth of carving can also be greater because of these overlays, giving the bold look that is typical of the design of this horse.

Head

3. Drill 2 × 1¼in(32mm) diameter eye sockets ¹⁄₁₆in(2mm) deep. In other words, just deep enough to give a clear outline as to where the eyes will be fitted later.

Cheek

5. Cut and glue overlays into position. The overlays on the cheeks allow room to include the quite deep indentation above the eye towards the forehead and another long shallow one by the temple, reaching from the corner of the eye and up towards the back of the ear. The cheek can be sloped very gently starting level with the eyes downwards until it ends in the very sharp dip at the lower end to 3in(76mm) wide at the back of the mouth. Having more room to manoeuvre tools there can be further carving within the mouth to form, with a gouge, a palate at the top.

11. The teeth in the lower jaw are cut away at the sides to show only ¼in(6mm) in height and a ¼in(6mm) in breadth which leaves a raised lump of wood in the middle which can be rounded at the edges to form a tongue. A horse's tongue has no groove down the centre like ours. On the outside the throat can also be carved to emphasize the underneath of the cheek bones and the hollow of the outside of the gullet in between.

Ears

16. There should be a ⅞in(22mm) gap between the ears. Looking from the front, the bottom of the ears do not go straight across the head above the forehead but slope down each side of the head for about 1¼in(32mm). The inner edge of the front of the ears is curved at the bottom and

½in(13mm) wide, getting wider until they are 1in(25mm) wide 2in(51mm) up from the bottom, then they start to narrow and round off at the top being 3in(76mm) tall in all (*see* right).

17.   Not applicable to this horse.

21.   Glue two overlays, one large and one small, on each side of the neck, which allows for the graceful sloping of the sides of the neck to the body without having to chisel too much wood away (*see* below).

22.   Starting between the ears, the crest of the head and neck is made by gouging out each side so that it is only ¾in(19mm) across and runs down the neck for about 14in(356mm). This emphasizes the proud arch of the head and neck which in turn is enhanced by a horsehair mane on top.

24.   With the horse's head arched, the tendons running from the tip of the cheek along then curving down its neck would

Front view showing the shape of the ears and nose.

The large horse on the swinger stand with head partially carved and all the overlays in position.

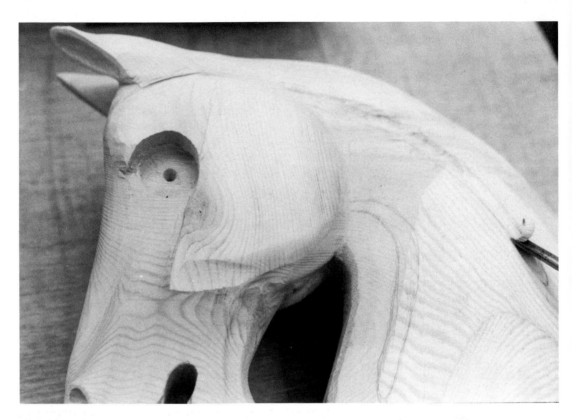

Chiselling the tendon grooves in the neck.

be showing and can be gouged out. Copy these from a photo of a horse because if they are not done correctly they only look like gouged-out channels in the neck. The position is very important and the sides of the grooves must be well rounded (*see* above).

Body

The middle section of the body consisting of the side and end planks should measure 29×9×5in(737×229×127mm) when glued together, plus the overlays which are cut out, planed and glued in the positions shown on the plans (*see* opposite, top), not forgetting the four little corner overlays that are glued into the corners next to the top of the outside leg overlays will be and

on the bottom plank side. They help to give a conformation of line between body and leg.

Before carving the underside of the body, fit, carve and sand the inside overlays on the legs so that the front and back of the underside of the horse can be carved and sanded right up to them.

Legs

Use the instructions for the legs in the chapter on a medium horse with these additions: the hooves do need the thickness of the overlays which are glued on to each side, otherwise they would look rather spindly compared to the rest of the horse. Shoes could be carved into the back

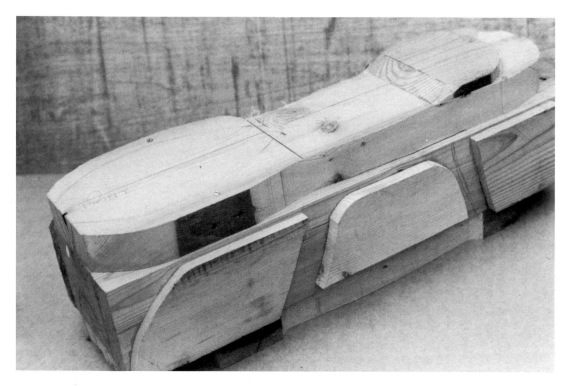

The large body with overlays glued on.

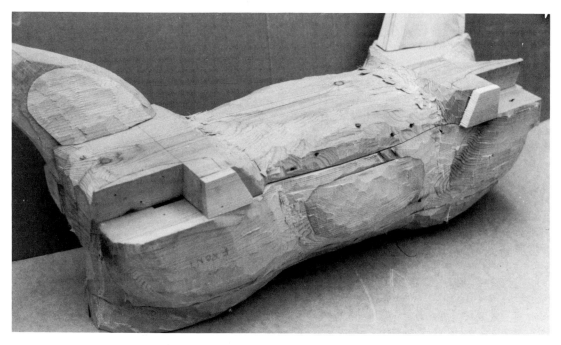

Side, bottom plank and inside leg carving details.

hooves but the underside of the front hooves are not seen.

Assembly

Use the instructions for the assembly in the chapter on a medium horse and add to instruction 8. Towards the top of the front legs there are two sinew grooves that go right up to the bunched body muscle and are surrounded by muscle. These show up quite clearly and are completely different from the back legs where the muscle is thick right across, except for the hamstring at the back and only shows a slight dip between leg and body muscles (*see* below and opposite).

Stand

The method of construction for the swinger stand of this horse is exactly the same as that used for the medium horse. Use the charts provided on pages 60–4 to get the sizes correct, and the instructions for the medium swinger stand. The only difference between them is that the fittings on this horse are shown in brass or brass plated, whereas the medium horse has black painted fittings.

Finishes

Different types of finishes are explained in 'Finishes', on page 65. One addition is

Ready for the final sanding.

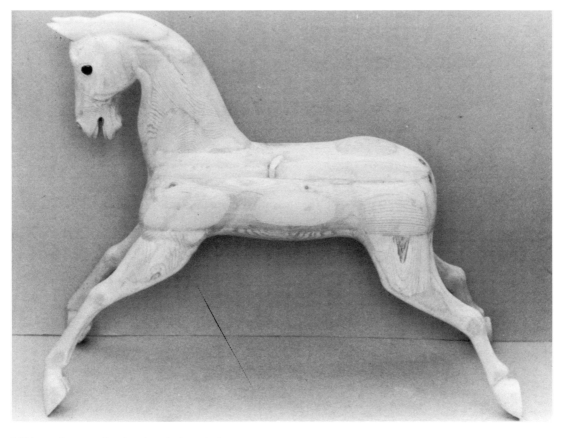

With sanding completed and ready for painting.

that because of the extra carving in the mouth the tops of the individual teeth can be painted as well as the sides, but remember that there will still only be four teeth showing each side, which makes a total of eight teeth in each of the upper and lower jaws.

The patterns for the large rocking horse on a swinger stand are on pages 118–21. (Scale 1:4.35.)

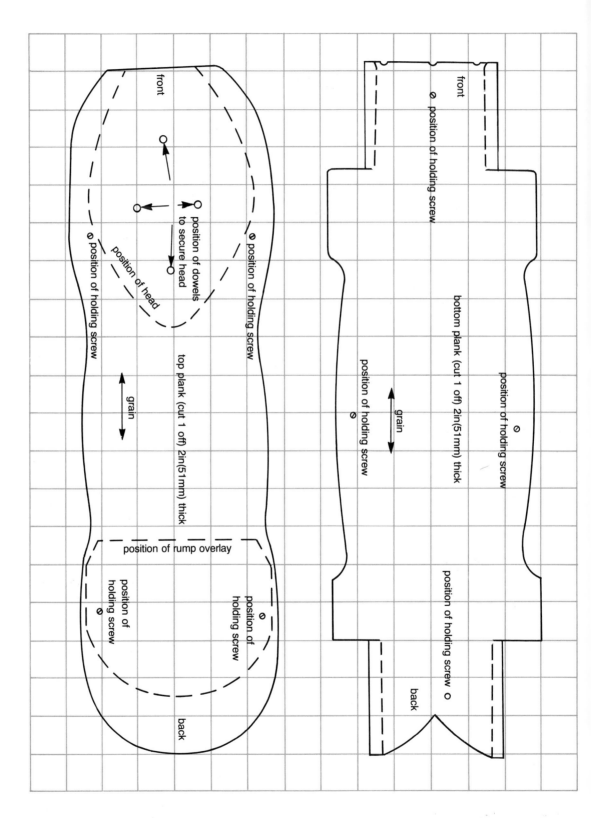

front

⊘ position of holding screw

position of dowels
to secure head

position of head

⊘ position of holding screw

position of holding screw

⊘ position of holding screw

grain

top plank (cut 1 off) 2in(51mm) thick

position of rump overlay

position of
holding screw

position of
holding screw

position of
holding screw

back

front

⊘ position of holding screw

position of holding screw

bottom plank (cut 1 off) 2in(51mm) thick

position of holding screw

grain

position of holding screw o

back

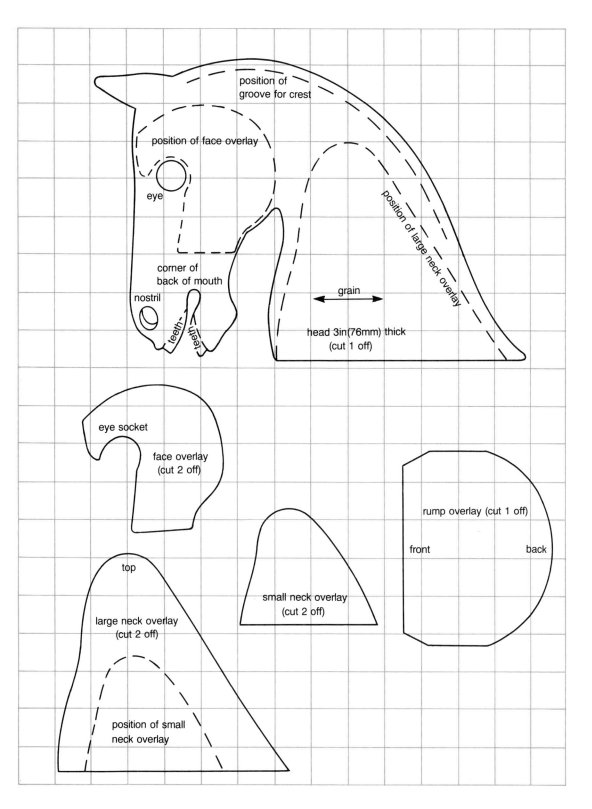

position of
groove for crest

position of face overlay

eye

corner of
back of mouth

nostril

teeth

teeth

grain

position of large neck overlay

head 3in(76mm) thick
(cut 1 off)

eye socket

face overlay
(cut 2 off)

rump overlay (cut 1 off)

front   back

top

large neck overlay
(cut 2 off)

small neck overlay
(cut 2 off)

position of small
neck overlay

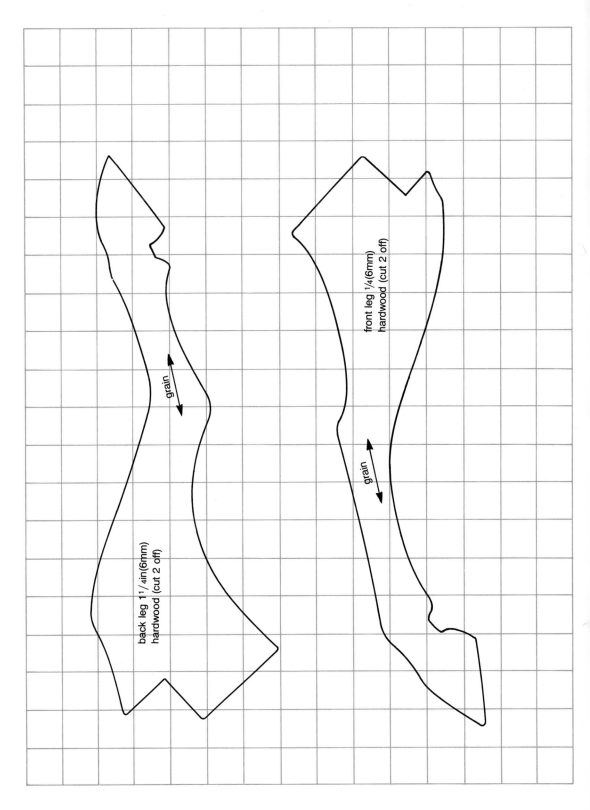

front leg ¹/₄(6mm)
hardwood (cut 2 off)

grain

back leg 1¹/₄in(6mm)
hardwood (cut 2 off)

grain

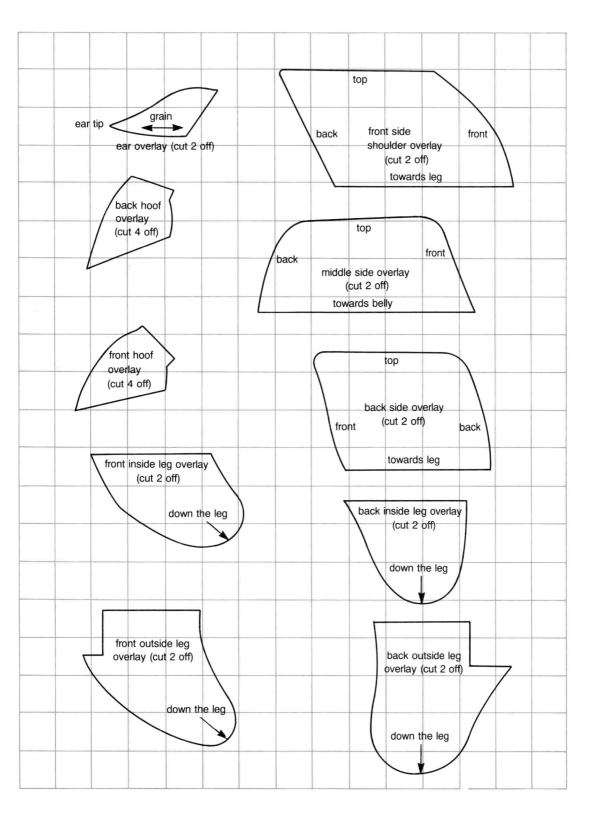

LARGE HORSE ON ROCKERS

This should be a dream of a horse, beautiful to behold as an ornament to grace any home, but equally practical as the ultimate toy that is never outgrown by any generation and perfect as the family heirloom everyone will love and treasure through many years.

The largest of the rocking horses, it is strongly reminiscent of the early to mid-nineteenth-century horses, the biggest difference being that the rockers are not nearly so high. This is for the riders' safety, causing them to stop and slide rather than tip at the end of a vigorous rock. The boat shape and centre box has been kept and the horse itself is stretched out as for a full gallop with its head more forward than any of the other sizes of horse.

This is a horse that needs space, both to show off the way that the curve of the rockers is reflected in the curve of the legs and body giving it a pleasing symmetry, and also for the practical reason that the rockers are 7ft(2.13m) long. On top of the length there has to be room for movement, so a minimum of 12ft(3.65m) long is needed for the horse to be used to its full potential. It is designed to last and is strongly built, which also means it is heavy. Moving the rocking horse about from one location to another needs handling by two people.

With the rocker model the proportions and carving can be shown off to better effect than those with a swinger stand where the elegant lines can be spoilt by parts of the stand which are positioned between the horse's legs. The rocking motion is not so smooth as the glide that swinger bars give but it is a more realistic ride; you can almost feel the hooves hitting the ground as you ride, because of having the same movement as a horse at full gallop which was so important when this type of horse was first created, to teach the rudiments of riding. Many adults enjoy a ride on these rocking horses, and provided it is treated with respect and the rider is not too heavy, the horse will come to no harm.

Having no moving parts, in other words the whole rocking horse and stand move as one item, there is no friction which causes wear as with a horse on a swinger stand. Therefore the only causes of deterioration are sheer hard use. It will stand plenty of that, misuse (and no maker can guard against it), or neglect. It is safe to say that as much restoration is needed because of neglect as is ever needed for just hard use.

The workshop needs to be big and high enough to manoeuvre the horse and especially the 7ft(2.13m) rockers in the last stages of construction and painting. There is a difference in the design of this horse because of the long gait, the front legs extend forwards from the corners of the bottom plank instead of downwards and then forwards from underneath as all the other horses do. It is not suitable in this size to go on a swinger stand because of the stretched-out stance and the placing of the legs which would mean the length of the swinger bars and stand would need to be out of all proportion to the size of the horse. The rock would have to be kept short if the centre of gravity, and therefore the stability of the horse is to be kept at a reasonable low level.

Each of the rockers is made in two halves so that the grain of the wood can be kept as long as possible at the ends of each half of the rocker. The rockers are boat shaped as well as bowed, being wide across the middle and narrow at both ends, therefore the two actual rockers are leaning inwards and the only part that touches the floor is the inner under edge. All parts of the middle box section must be well above this inner edge when installed to allow the edge of the rockers to be well rounded.

Dimensions

At 53in(1,346mm) high, 38in(965mm) to the top of the saddle and 32in(812mm) from breast to rump grading it as a large horse, it stands on 7ft(2,133mm) long rockers, 21in(533mm) at the widest point. (All these measurements are approximate.)

Detail of breast, neck and head when sanding is complete.

Time

It takes a minimum of sixty hours to make plus drying time for glue and paint.

Tools

The same tools are required as for the medium horse except that sash clamp lengths are 19in(483mm) long, a vice is needed and 1½in(39mm) spade bit.

Materials

If the main head piece is to be made out of two pieces of 3in(76mm) thick wood because of the width required, the join should be made in the top end of the head somewhere about forehead level and not at the bottom end which would mean a join somewhere in the nose. The join should be securely dowelled. A join in the wood of a head can be seen on page 41 (top).

Horse

Head: 1 × softwood
22×17×3in(559×432×76mm)
Top plank: 1 × softwood
32×9½×2in(813×241×51mm)
Side plank: 2 × softwood 32×6×2in(813× 152× 51mm)
Bottom plank: 1 × softwood 32×10×2in(813× 254× 51mm)
End plank: 2 × softwood
6×6×3in(152×152×76mm)
Front leg: 2 × hardwood
37×10½×1½in(940×267×38mm) if both are cut from the same piece of wood
Back leg: 2 × hardwood
39×9×1½in(991×229×38mm) as above
Screws countersink: 12 × 2in(51mm) No. 8, 12 × 2½in(64mm) No. 8
Eyes glass, brown iris: 2 × 1⅛in(28mm) diameter

Given below are the sizes of the pieces of wood that are needed if every overlay is to be cut individually.

> Overlays: measurements are all length × width × thickness
> Ears: 2 × 1½×3×¼in(38×76×6mm)
> Cheek: 2 x 7×7×⅜in(178×178×9mm)
> Large neck: 2 × 8×11×1¼in (203×279×32mm)
> Small neck: 2 × 3×7¼×1in(76×184×25mm)
> Shoulder: 2 × 8½×7¼×½in (216×184× 13mm)
> Ribs: 2 × 5¼×10½×½in(133×267×13mm)
> Side rump: 2 × 11×5¼×½in (279×133×13mm)
> Top rump: 1 × 11×7×1in(279×178×25mm)
> Inside leg front (1): 2 × 6×3×½in (152×76×13mm)
> Inside leg front (2): 2 x 5×2×½in (127× 51×13mm)
> Inside leg back: 2 × 8½×3×½in (216×76×13mm)
> Outside leg front: 2 × 5¾×7×1½in (146×178×38mm)
> Outside leg back: 2 × 5½×7×1¼in (141×178×32mm)
> Hooves front: 4 × 4½×3½×½in (114×89×13mm)
> Hooves back: 4 × 4½×4×½in (114×102×13mm)

The four parts of the rockers need a wide piece of wood so two of the three pieces might have to be used. Incorporating the legs in the same pieces of wood may mean that the overall amount required is reduced.

Rockers

> Rockers: 4 × 43×7¾×1½in (1,092×197× 38mm)
> Spacer bars: 2 × 12in(305mm) long and 2in(51mm) diameter
> Box side: 2 × 16¼×2¼×1in (413× 57×25mm)
> Box end: 2 × 16½×2¼×¾in (419×57×19mm)
> Box planks: 7 × 21in(533mm) long approximately 3in(76mm) wide
> Roofing bolts: 4 × M6 and the length is decided after the horse is made
> End caps: 4 × metal 1⅝in(41mm) diameter ½in(13mm) deep (optional)

Accessories

Mane and tail, bridle, reins, saddle, stirrups, stirrup-straps, numnah or saddle cloth, martingale, cropper strap. Except for the mane and tail, all or some of these can enhance the horse and the choice is wide, details of which are in Chapter 4. Although a decision on what type of saddle is going to be used should be made before commencing carving, if the saddle is to be removable, provision needs to be made for this.

Construction

The same instructions can be followed as for the large horse on a swinger stand which is at the beginning of this chapter, except for some small variations. These are that the front leg sockets are cut on an angle, part of which is already cut away on the side planks of the body. The socket needs deepening at the front (*see* opposite, top) as shown in the diagram and table on pages 45–6 with the accompanying chart giving the measurements. Likewise the sockets for the back legs are partly cut out too. These cuts need to go deeper and include the middle plank which is screwed into position to facilitate this as shown in the diagram and table on pages 45–6.

There are three overlays down each side of the body and one on the top plank. Glue these into position after the middle section has been glued together and the leg sockets cut out, but before any carving is done. The small corner overlays used on the large horse on swinger bars are not used on this horse, but the inside front leg overlays are in two parts which are butted together over the front corners of the bottom plank as indicated on the plans.

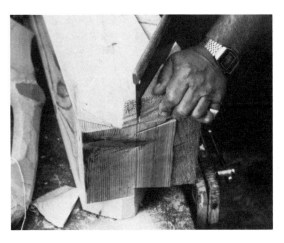

One way of sawing out the front leg sockets.

Showing the muscles of the legs and body.

Carving

The horse is at full gallop and the position of the muscles in the body section should show this. The muscles above the front legs are very bunched and follow through the line of the leg right up to the withers (*see* page 125 and below). The back legs are stretched out, accordingly the back muscles show the long lines of muscles stretching from back legs and well up into the side of the horse. Another point where the galloping stance of the horse can be emphasized is in the grooves on the stretched neck where the tendons show up, espe-

Showing the body curves and the way the neck muscles slope into the top of the leg muscles.

cially the one from the top of the cheek which should be streamlined and not curving downwards to the same extent as on a trotting horse. There should also be a long sloping rump. If you are unsure, photographic reference from a book on horse-riding proves useful.

Head, Cheek, Ears and Neck

To avoid duplication follow the instructions for the large horse on a swinger stand at the beginning of this chapter.

Assembly

Plane the bottom of the head, glue and screw it into position on the top plank, then change the screws for dowels. Glue and screw or clamp the middle hollow section to the bottom plank and allow it to dry. Glue and screw the legs into their sockets and when dry, replace the screws with dowels. For further details, *see* the assembly section in Chapter 5, Points 1 and 4–7. Leave the horse at this stage until the rockers are made.

Rockers

1. Cut out the four halves of the rockers very carefully. It is important that all four should match well, especially along the bottom of each rocker. The line of the cut at the end should be perfectly square and straight as it becomes the join in the middle of the rocker.
2. Plane the flat sides.
3. Using a large flat surface such as the floor, butt two halves of the rocker together. Lay the other two halves on top and butt together. The four halves should match perfectly. If they do not, adjustment can be made to the join by shaving off

> **Tip** If more than one set of rockers is to be made of these dimensions, a jig can be made to stop any movement of the rockers.

small amounts of wood. It is very important that the four halves match all the way along, as only small inconsistencies can be planed or sanded away.

4. Cut out the side and end pieces of the middle box section, plane all flat sides and the bottom longer edge of the two end pieces. Cut off the top two corners of the end pieces, making an angle of 80° so that the top edge is 15¾in(400mm) long.

5. On the two curved side pieces, mark the centre and drill where indicated eight holes to take No. 8 screws. Chamfer ¼in (6mm) off the two lower outside edges.

6. With centre and top edges matching, place one side piece in position across the centre of the top two rockers. On one side of the centre of the side piece, drill pilot holes through only two of the holes and screw in 1½in(38mm) No. 8 screws.

7. Check again that the butt join is as close as possible, then do the same with the other half of the side piece. By only using two holes on each side at first, if there has been any movement causing a slight mismatch there is a second chance of getting it right by using the other two screw holes on one or both sides. Only when you are satisfied that the butt join is as neat as possible are the other four pilot holes drilled and the screws put in.

8. Turn the whole of both rockers over and prop up the ends of the lower one so that it is perfectly flat. Use the same procedure as for Points 6 and 7, ensuring the rockers are well matched at all times.

9. When satisfied, clamp the two rockers together in four places. Unscrew only one side at a time and smear the inside with glue before screwing back on again.

10. When dry, the top and bottom of both rockers can be planed and sanded while still clamped together, ensuring that both will be identical. The bottom of the rockers should be very smooth with no humps or hollows, as each one will be felt by the rider.

11. The only exception is that the centre 6in(152mm) should be flat to aid the rider to mount. The ends of this 6in(152mm) should be gradually smoothed away.

12. The rockers can now be unclamped and all their edges sanded round, especially on the outside of the end curls and the inside bottom edge. The latter is the only part which makes contact with the floor, so there should not be even the slightest hint of a sharp edge. The end pieces of the box section can now be drilled and the rockers put together.

13. Clamp one rocker in a vice in an almost upright position with the box side piece on the outside ready for the other rocker to be attached next to it.

14. Along each of the short sides of one box end piece, two holes are drilled to take No. 8 screws. These holes slant outwards at about 45°so that when the box end piece is in place, the screws will bite into the hard rockers rather than the soft end grain of the curved side pieces. Countersink the holes.

15. Butt one end piece with the narrow length level with the top of the rocker and on to the end curved side piece.

16. Drill a pilot hole through the lower of the two holes and screw a 1½in(38mm) No. 8 countersink screw through the end piece and into the rocker (*see* overleaf).

17. Turn the rocker the other way up in

Box end plank being screwed to rocker and curved side plank.

the vice and screw the other end piece in place, using only one screw in the lower hole.

18. Screw the other end of the end pieces to the other rocker, using the vice to keep one rocker still.

19. The rockers are very vulnerable to twisting at this point, so clamp them across the top of the box section with two sash clamps. Take the rockers out of the vice and lay them on the floor right way up. The two rockers should now be boat shaped, slanting inwards, coming in narrow at both ends and wide where the box frame is attached.

20. Balance the horse on the rockers to check that the hooves have about half their width on the rocker and the other half overhanging the outside edge. If the rockers are too far apart, then the amount needed to bring them closer together is cut off one or both of the end pieces of the box. On the other hand, if the rockers are too

narrow, measure how much wider they need to be and make new end pieces for the box section longer by the extra amount required.

21. When the horse has balanced correctly, take it off and drill the remaining four pilot holes in the box end pieces, putting in the other four screws.

22. Lay the rockers on their side, then drill and countersink a hole to take a No. 12 screw vertically in each end curl as indicated. Turn the rockers over and do likewise in the other two end curls. These holes are off centre on the outside so that the other end will be within the circumference of the ends of the spacer bars.

The end spacer bars now need cutting to size. The end surfaces of these are on a slant, the angle of which is exactly the same as the slant of the box ends. This slant can be done quite quickly on a bandsaw with an adjustable bed. To measure the length of the spacer bar, measure first the distance between the two screw holes on the insides of the end scrolls of the rockers. This becomes the distance between the two centre points of the slants on the spacer bar.

> **Tip** If you feel you could easily get the measurements and slants wrong, do a dummy run with an odd piece of softwood that is about the same thickness.

Drill a pilot hole through the centre of each of the end slanting surfaces of the two spacer bars and screw them in place. Check that they fit correctly and then unscrew them, glue the end surfaces and screw them back into place.

Lastly the boards are screwed to the top surface of the rockers, completing the box. A point to watch when cutting out the boards is that the board in the centre will be the longest and the outside ones the shortest. Another point is that many riders use the box as a step up when mounting, and to accommodate this, the boards can overlap the rockers by no more than 1in(25mm) or they can be neatly cut off to follow the curve of the rockers. Plane top and both sides of the boards. Drill and screw with four 1¼in(32mm) No. 8 countersink screws each board to the rockers. Cover the screw tops with wood filler then sand down. Chamfer all four edges of the finished box top, rounding the corners for safety.

Alternative to boards is to use one sheet of plywood which must be thick enough to stand the weight of a child, particularly as very often the box section gets used as an extra seat.

When the rockers are complete, continue with medium horse instructions for legs Points 13–15, for assembly from Points 2–7 with one variation which is that as these large rockers are slanting, the rebates for all four hooves need cutting ¼in(6mm) wider than the vertical marker lines to accommodate the slant. Follow with assembly section details Points 8–11 and follow with the eyes and setting the eyes.

When the painting and dressing of the horse is complete, put it back on its rockers and adjust so that the head is not dipping forward, and finish as Points 12 and 13 of the medium horse assembly.

The patterns for the large rocking horse on bow rockers are on pages 130–3. (Scale 1:5.)

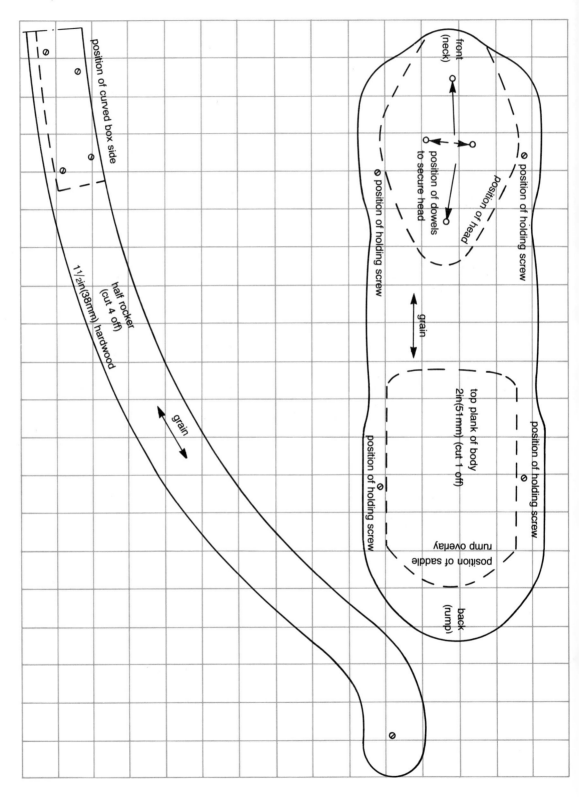

position of curved box side

position of dowels
to secure head

front
(neck)

position of holding screw

position of head

position of holding screw

grain

top plank of body
2in(51mm) (cut 1 off)

position of holding screw

position of saddle
rump overlay

back
(rump)

position of holding screw

half rocker
(cut 4 off)

1¹/₂in(38mm) hardwood

grain

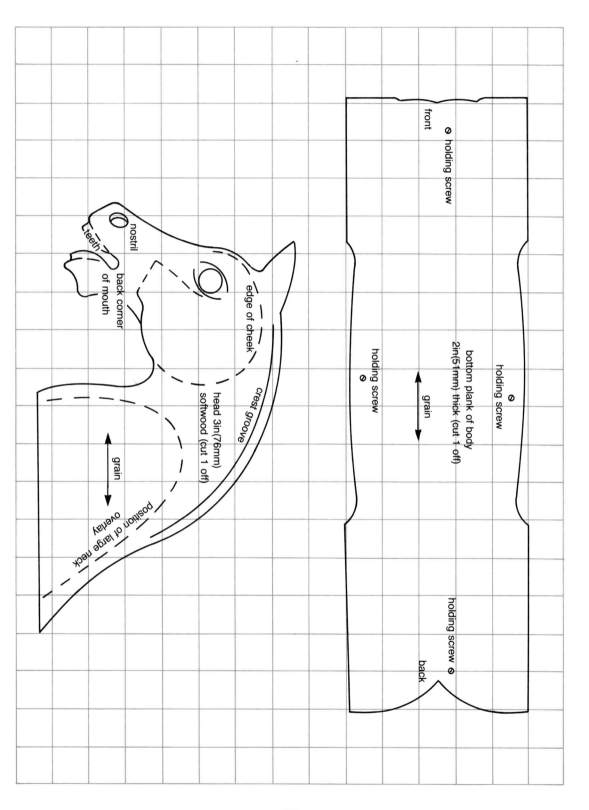

nostril

teeth

back corner
of mouth

edge of cheek

crest groove

head 3in(76mm)
softwood (cut 1 off)

grain

position of large neck
overlay

front

⊖ holding screw

bottom plank of body
2in(51mm) thick (cut 1 off)

holding screw
⊖

holding screw
⊖

grain

holding screw ⊖
back

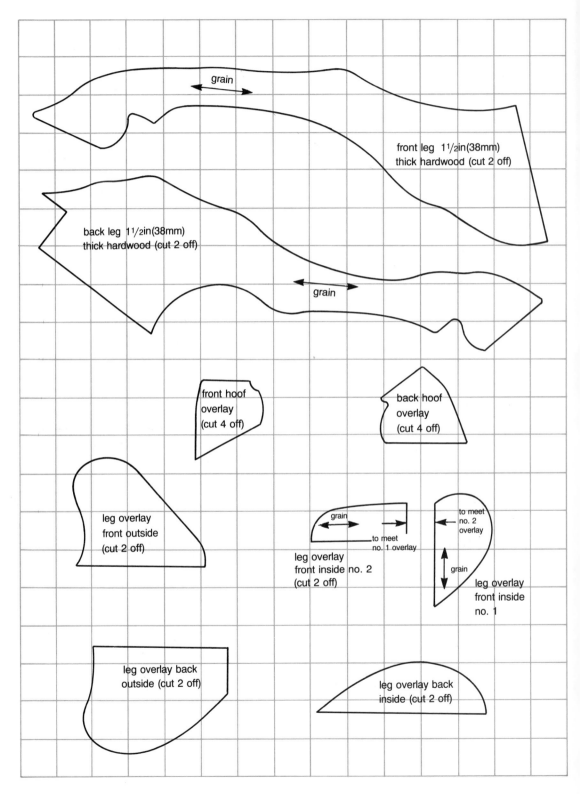

grain

front leg 1 1/2 in (38mm)
thick hardwood (cut 2 off)

back leg 1 1/2 in (38mm)
thick hardwood (cut 2 off)

grain

front hoof
overlay
(cut 4 off)

back hoof
overlay
(cut 4 off)

leg overlay
front outside
(cut 2 off)

grain

to meet
no. 1 overlay

leg overlay
front inside no. 2
(cut 2 off)

to meet
no. 2
overlay

grain

leg overlay
front inside
no. 1

leg overlay back
outside (cut 2 off)

leg overlay back
inside (cut 2 off)

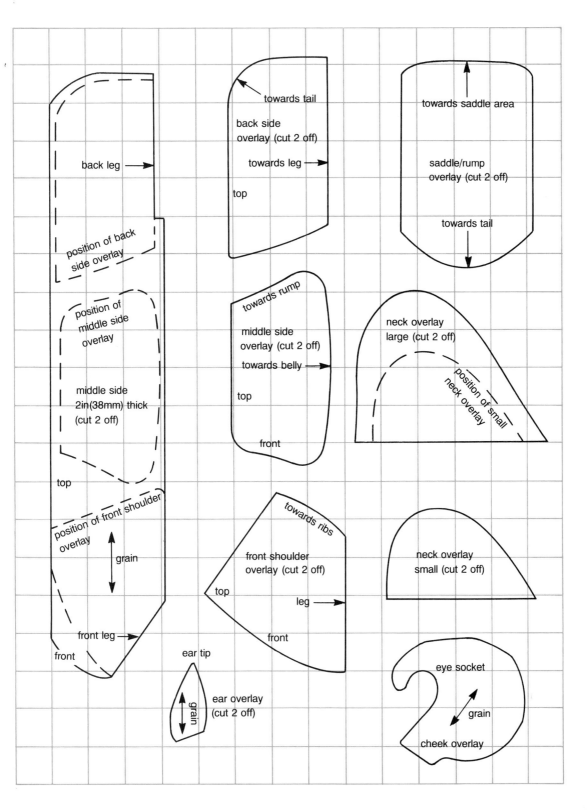

towards tail

back side
overlay (cut 2 off)

towards leg →

top

towards saddle area

saddle/rump
overlay (cut 2 off)

towards tail

back leg →

position of back
side overlay

position of
middle side
overlay

middle side
2in(38mm) thick
(cut 2 off)

top

position of front shoulder
overlay

grain

front leg →

front

towards rump

middle side
overlay (cut 2 off)

towards belly →

top

front

neck overlay
large (cut 2 off)

position of small
neck overlay

towards ribs

front shoulder
overlay (cut 2 off)

top

leg →

front

neck overlay
small (cut 2 off)

ear tip

ear overlay
(cut 2 off)

grain

eye socket

grain

cheek overlay

CHAPTER TEN

RESTORATION

The reason behind restoring a rocking horse is to make it usable. For example, if it is going into a museum it needs to be in a condition where it does not fall to pieces every time it is moved. However, museums do not want rocking horses that have undergone reconditioning, the nearer they are to the original condition, the better. It needs some detective work, both to discover how old the horse is and whether its coat of paint is the original one.

Apart from very small horses, pre-1920 horses have a pummel hole for side-saddle riding at each side of the front end of the saddle. There is also a wooden back-rest to this type of saddle. A layer of plaster called gesso lies between the wood of the horse and the paint and covers the whole of the body and head. The nostrils are rounded and flared. Horses from the late 1870s onwards may be on swinger stands with black painted iron fitments. Pre- and early-1870s horses are on deep boat-shaped rockers which are most likely painted dark green. The end spacer bars are about 1½in(38mm) diameter, of turned wood and there is a platform in the middle of the rockers (which were made in two halves). This platform should be made of between five and seven strips of softwood about 3in(76mm) wide and overlapping the rocker sides by about 1in(25mm). The platform should show wear marks.

Turn the rockers upside down and underneath the platform are four shaped pieces of softwood that are nailed into position to form an open box; they hold the two halves of the rockers together and cross from one rocker side to the other. The underside was never painted and is usually the first place to get boring insect infestation and rot, so a close inspection is necessary and preventative measures, such as spraying, is a good idea. From about the 1840s onwards the horses are dapple greys. The finishing coat of paint is a light grey/blue. First of all the dappling was very skilfully stippled on by hand and could be on any part of the body as the earliest horses were very individual, having been made by hand. Gradually the dappling became more stylized until by the twentieth century most, but not all, horses just had small patches of dapple on each side of the rump, the round of the belly, the round of the muscle above the forelegs and each side of the neck. Over the dapple there was painted a protective coat of clear varnish, but this, like that on old paintings, becomes discoloured with time, so by now the patches where the varnish is complete give a very yellow appearance to the horse.

Before about 1840 the appearance of the rocking horses reflect those of real horses in the paintings of the same period, for instance those which show hunting scenes. The legs and necks are stretched out, but the stance is very stiff. Ears are very small, mouths narrow – especially the bottom lip. The whole appearance is that of a slender horse with not many curves on the legs, but very often a finely carved head. It is rare to find a horse of this age that has not been restored. Indeed most have been restored many times. The colour should be plain or spotted, black on a pale grey/blue background.

The hooves do not have rebates so they do not sit partly on top of the rocker, and instead are bolted to the sides of the rockers (*see* right). These bolts usually have bent over the years and are very hard to remove – very often they have to be sawn through to get the horse off. This idea of bolting the hooves to the sides of the rockers was used up until about 1880.

Any of the above rocking horses would be considered by museums to fill gaps in their collections, but only if they were in original condition. The only restoration carried out would be to treat for such things as woodworm and rot, careful cleaning of the paint with a non-abrasive paint cleaner and the application of leather restorer to leather work.

Limbs may be glued back into position if they have fallen off, but if you are giving a rocking horse to a museum it is best to follow their instructions. These horses will never be ridden, but are used as a point of reference for anyone who wants to know how they looked and were made long ago, so the more authentic they are the better.

On the other hand an old and worn out rocking horse that has served a family well for generations and has come to the point where the next generation is due to use it, should carefully be restored so that it is safe to use and is able to give service for

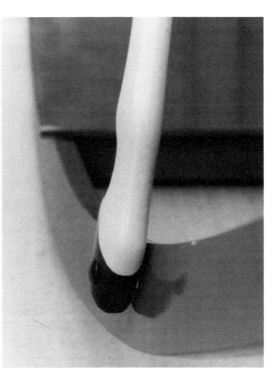

The original way of bolting the hoof to the side of the rocker instead of having a rebate.

many more years to come. This is the type of job we are aiming at with the restoration instructions in this book.

Providing a rocking horse is not eaten away with worm and falling apart with wet or dry rot *all over*, it can be restored so that it is fit for use, but it will not necessarily look exactly as it would have done originally. Unless you are proficient in woodcarving, carpentry, have a wide knowledge of how a rocking horse is made and are used to restoring, it may be wiser to allow an expert to do any major work on the horse. It is very easy to do a great deal of damage and cause much more work unnecessarily when trying to do what appears to be a small repair. However, this chapter gives details of the majority of repairs that you may need to carry out. By following these instructions most horses can be restored, depending of course on the ability of the restorer and time available.

Apart from new mane, tail and tack (*see* Chapter 4), before any restoration is done on a rocking horse a close examination of all parts of the horse should be made to see what must be done, what could be done and what should be better left alone. Therefore please read the appropriate sections first before actually starting. It might save you a great deal of unnecessary work,

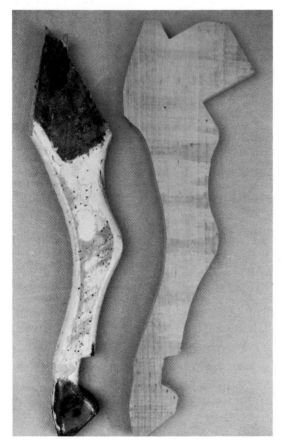

The first shape of a new leg including the missing tenon and a piece at the top of the leg. A good example of woodworm blow holes.

as more harm than good can be done by an overenthusiastic amateur.

It is important before doing anything at all to make a clear record of how it should look by taking some photographs. Memories have a bad habit of playing tricks. On the other hand photographs may show up what a good job you have made of an absolute wreck.

BRASS ROSETTES AND OTHER TRIM

When taking any tack off an old horse, do make sure to keep it all together. This practice, apart from keeping the workshop tidy, assists when refitting or checking on size, shape or colour of the original. *Do not throw anything away* until the restoration is complete. Any fancy rosettes or name plates should carefully be lifted off by inserting a screw driver blade under the rosette and the leather or material behind it, and slowly twisting the blade, hopefully lifting the rosette off. Diagrams should be made of their original position, so that as many as possible can be returned to same place at the end of the restoration. Remember such things as these brass rosettes, if there are any, are part of the horse's pedigree, because they are one of the indicators of the period in which the horse was originally made.

WOODWORM

The first thing to look for is insect infestation, for example woodworm, which is indicated by very tiny, perfectly round holes called blow holes (*see* left). If wood dust comes out of the holes there is still live woodworm inside. The trouble with this problem is that each hole shows where the grub has been chewing away inside the wood for a year or more. It only chews through the surface when it becomes a mature insect and flies away to mate. It returns briefly to a piece of wood to lay its eggs in a crack, or even an old blow hole, to start the whole process over again. The destruction inside the wood is many, many times more than shows on the surface. There are many brands of insecticide that will kill any insects that are still lurking, but once the damage has been done, the affected area should be renewed, especially anywhere where there is strain when the horse is in use, such as the legs, leg joints, rockers, stand pillars or hoof rail. Many other wood-boring insects have the same life-cycle.

OLD PAINT AND GESSO

Many horses have been overpainted at some time. In the majority of cases it is a member of the family who has put on 'a lick of paint' to smarten the old horse up, and possibly hammered in a few nails at the same time to secure a loose joint. The old paint and gesso is rarely removed first, so it is possible to see under the last coat of paint, where patches of gesso have come off and just been painted over. If you want to go back to the original colours, try to pick little pieces off the newer coat of paint and find the layer of original paint underneath. If you are lucky you can detect if part of the body had dappling and if it had, what type and how much. Before starting the main stripping, make a sketch of where the dappling is and get your paint mixed to give the right pale grey/blue colour. Disregard the yellowing coat of varnish on top, unless you want to apply yellowed, clear varnish to match.

Sometimes the paintwork is fairly good and the joints sound, in which case careful patching up of the knocks where paint and gesso has come away is all that may be needed. To do this, clean the paintwork first with a good paint cleaner and then remove any loose paint and gesso (after mixing the paint to match in colour). Mix up a small amount of gesso (for details see 'Gesso' on page 66). Dab the area to be repaired with cold water on a very small paint brush, then, with a knife, press in the thick gesso. Anything that is larger than $\frac{3}{4}$in(19mm) diameter will need the gesso putting on in two coats, allowing the first to dry before the second is put on. The gesso, when it is applied, should be slightly higher than the surrounding paintwork, in order that a gentle sand with fine paper will bring it flat with the surround without there being any ridges or dips.

Using very small brushes, apply a coat of sealer, lightly sand this with fine sandpaper when dry, follow with a coat of primer and a coat of undercoat, allowing them to dry thoroughly each time. The final top coat of paint overlaps the edges of the other coats and fades into nothing all round. This can be achieved by loading the brush with smaller amounts of paint, or alternatively, by smoothing it very gently with the fingertips, or dipping the very tip of the paint brush in paint thinner and brushing around the edges. Considerable care must be taken with the last method as too much thinners will cause drips across the paint. Dapple to match (see which type in Chapter 5 under heading 'Dappling') if it is needed and then you can apply clear varnish or tint the varnish with just a little light oak varnish to give it the old yellow appearance, if this is what is desired.

STRIPPING

If the horse's paint is very badly chipped or it has been overpainted and there is other work to be done (such as loose joints and cracks) it is better to sand off all the paint and gesso and start from scratch.

Ordinary paint stripper does not have much effect on gesso and although dipping the horse in a tank of caustic stripper does get all the paint and gesso off, it has an adverse effect on the top layer of the wood. It also takes months for the horse to dry out properly, as this has to be done very slowly to avoid further cracking of the wood. The most effective method is to sand it off with sanding discs on the correct attachment for a hand-held drill, the awkward corners being cleaned out by using rifler files. The whole process of sanding is very messy and is best done in the open air if no dust extractors are available. Always wear a dust mask when carrying out this work.

DRY ROT

This cannot always be seen (especially when it is confined only to a small area) before the paint and gesso have been removed. The middle of the infected wood is discoloured and soft, and cracks into segments similar to little bricks in a wall. It is very insidious because it is a fungus infection, which means that apart from the area of discoloured wood (which is in an advanced state of deterioration) the spoors of the fungus will already be working on a great deal of the surrounding wood which looks perfectly sound. Unless this area is treated as well as the rotten wood renewed, the fungus will continue to spread. Treat the wood with a dry rot

preventative fluid to the extent required by the instructions on the can.

WET ROT

This results when wood has remained wet for some considerable time, and makes it discoloured. Dig your fingernails into affected areas – it will feel spongy and crumble. All affected areas need replacing. As dry rot usually affects areas that have wet rot it is wise to treat all the surrounding wood with preventative fluid, as you would for dry rot.

CONSTRUCTION

It is very tempting to take the whole horse apart to see how it is constructed, but as with a watch mechanism, it is easier to take apart than it is to put back together again correctly. The basic construction of the horse itself is a hollow box for a body and a solid head, both of which were made of a good quality softwood – usually pine. The solid legs needed to be a hardwood and traditionally would have been attached to the body by mortice and tenon joints. All pre-1940 horses were glued together with animal glue and almost all were also nailed. Some makers put scrim (a coarse weave cotton cloth) over all the leg joints, presumably to help stop them cracking and coming loose. In time, however, this made no difference, and the joints cracked open just as frequently as any of the others. In the nineteenth century and the beginning of the twentieth century, horses were constructed with a hole each side at the front end of the saddle area. These holes were for banana-shaped pummels (*see* page 155) to be pushed in so that the girls could hook their leg round them when they were riding side-saddle. The pummels could be easily removed again when the boys rode astride, which meant that most were lost. The holes go right through to the hollow centre of the body and were used by the children to 'post' things into the horse, so very often an old horse will rattle. Usually the treasures inside are such things as marbles, lead soldiers and pencils, but sometimes more exotic things, such as silver tea spoons and silver thimbles are recovered, or just unusual items, such as two and a half yards of table lamp flex or a war time bill for biscuits, including the amount of ration points needed!

SPLITS AND CRACKS

Most splits and cracks in the head and body are caused by the horse being in a damp atmosphere for a very long time, such as an attic, garage or even an unheated room and then brought into the dry atmosphere created by central heating or air-conditioning. The wood dries out and shrinks too quickly and the cracks appear. If the cracks and splits are large and the edges can be made to move, then any dirt or gesso should be cleaned out and a sliver of wood, of the same type if possible, cut to size and smeared with glue and pushed into the fault. The sliver of wood should go in as deep as possible. If the crack is too fine to get a sliver of wood in, but there is movement, open out the crack by sawing a slot that is just the width of the saw blade along the line of the crack and at least ¼in(6mm) deep to take the sliver of wood. Only hairline cracks that have no movement are filled with wood filler. The sliver of wood should only be a push tight fit. Do

not force it in or you will make the split even larger!

Sometimes the joins in the body section come apart. This could be where the wood was not fully seasoned when the horse was made and has subsequently warped (a problem that very often occurs with the neck overlays). This usually means that the horse will have to come apart at that point and the surfaces be planed flat before re-gluing and clamping into position. Beware of nails that will ruin your planer blade. Gluing and clamping this type of crack without planing doesn't work; the edges just spring apart again. With the neck overlays it is difficult to get a clamp to stay on, after smearing with glue, so screw the wood in place. Withdraw the screws when dry. As there is no stress on these pieces of wood, the holes left by the screws can be filled with wood filler.

Another reason for the body joins coming apart can be damp. The old glues used were water soluble, so too much damp and they just dissolve away. All that is needed in this case is to clean the surfaces of the joins, smear with glue and clamp them together to dry, or screw if clamps won't fit. To ensure that the same thing doesn't happen again, take away the clamps and screws when the joins are dry and put in ⅜in(9mm) dowels at strategic points.

NAILS AND SCREWS

Most old horses were nailed together with square nails which had oblong heads. The neck and leg overlays were glued in place. From about the 1920s round or oval nails with round heads were used and the neck and leg overlays were nailed in place with small pin nails. Later still some horses were screwed together. Screws were used mainly to screw the cross planks and end stops into place on the swinger stands or the end spacer bars on the bow rockers. Early ones would have had the square nails. These nails can still be purchased so they are not an infallible guide to age. The disadvantage of nails and screws it that they rust easily, which discolours and rots the wood in the immediate locality, or the nail or screw expands with rust, making it almost impossible to remove. Very often this causes breaking just below the head, making removal even more difficult.

Sometimes the horse has already been repaired at least once before, and there will be more nails or screws added in an attempt to keep breaks and joins together. This second crop of nails or screws almost always are very large and long. At this point some detective work is needed to locate the heads of the right nails or screws and a decision made as to which must be removed to make an effective repair and which, if they are removed, will cause too much damage by cracking the wood or requiring lumps of wood to be gouged out to get at them. The rule of thumb is, if the nail or screw is the only thing that is keeping two parts together, then it will have to come out to allow the surfaces to be cleaned, glued and otherwise prepared, but if there is only slight movement and the parts are partially glued together, leave well alone and look for other methods of getting the rest of the area sound.

THE SEPARATE PARTS OF THE HORSE

Leg Joint

The most common point of all for cracking is at the top of the legs where the tenon of the leg goes into the mortice of the bottom plank of the body. This is sometimes caused by a badly cut joint so that the glue just has not made contact with all the surfaces, by damp, or by a misfit where the hoof is bolted to the hoof rail causing movement in the leg, but usually it is caused by normal hard wear. Again if the joint is only partially cracked and there are rusty nails holding it, to try and take out the nails and free the joint would very likely chew up the surrounding wood so much that new sections might have to be put in, so this is a case of 'best left alone'. Treat it as a crack and deal with it as detailed in the section on splits and cracks.

If the leg is really wobbly, even if there are rusty nails, the nails will have to come out and the leg be taken out, but unless they are loose only take out the nails that are affecting the leg. Clean off all the old glue, being careful not to take any wood away with the glue, both on the tenon and in the mortice and remove all dirt and old gesso. Try the leg back into position with the hoof bolted into the hoof rail. This is to make sure that the mortice and tenon are seated correctly and the horse is standing on its rockers upright, or if it is on swinger bars, that these are free to move between the legs. If all is well, unbolt the horse, take the joint apart, apply the glue and put the tenon back into the mortice. Bolt the horse back on its rockers or hoof rails while the glue is setting, otherwise you might find that the leg isn't at exactly the same angle as it was originally and doesn't match the holes in the hoof rail, or worse still misses the rocker or hoof rail altogether. The latter can happen if the original mortice and tenon was not a good fit to start with. For a leg joint that does not fit together properly, after the old glue etc., has been removed, fit the leg into the body as before and bolt all four legs to rocker or hoof rail. Make wedges of the same wood as the body to fit exactly into the gaps where the mortice and tenon joint are mismatched. When you are sure that there are enough wedges prepared, take it all apart as before, apply the glue, assemble it and bolt it on to the rockers or hoof rails. Then check that the swinger bars move freely and the horse is quite upright (a spirit level across the horses back will help), and push the wedges, smeared with glue, into place and leave it all in position where it won't be disturbed to dry. When the leg joint is solid again, to give it extra strength put in dowels (*see* below). One ¼in(6mm) dowel for a small horse and two ⅜in(9mm)

dowels in medium and large horses. The dowels should go through the part of the side of the body that is over the mortice slot, through the tenon, which is in the mortice and into the bottom plank the other side. Remove any protruding pieces of wood and you have a good firm joint ready for sanding.

New Leg

Splits in the wood of an actual leg or where the hole is for the hoof to be bolted to the stand, shows the start of trouble that can only get worse. This is the part of the horse where it is not advisable to splice in new wood. This applies also to any signs of

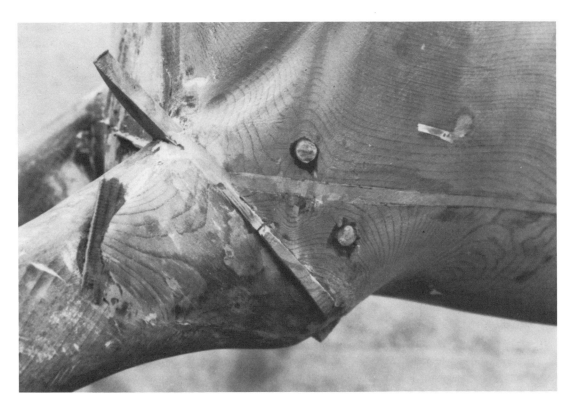

Slivers of wood put in the cleaned-out cracks and the dowels inserted to strengthen the join.

wood worm or rot. A whole new leg should be made; there is too much strain on the legs to do just a cosmetic repair. A break in a leg while a child is riding could be disastrous.

To cut out a new leg, use a piece of wood of the same type as the old leg and as thick as the thickest part, not including the muscle (overlay) which is glued to the top of the leg next to the body. Lay the old leg flat side of the tenon against the wood, making sure that the grain of the wood is along the length of the leg. Draw round the leg, making sure that your pencil is vertical all the time to ensure that the drawing is an exact copy. To make doubly sure, check the old leg and drawing with calipers to see that they correspond, but allow a small amount of extra size for sanding off.

If the leg is missing, or in too poor a condition to use as a copy, make a cardboard cut-out, including the tenon of the other leg of the pair. Again, check with calipers and also put it into the mortice to check the top is right. If both legs of a pair are missing, lay the horse on its side on cardboard, make a measurement from the bottom plank of the body to the tip of the legs that are there. Transfer this measurement to the area of the missing legs by drawing a straight line to indicate the edge of the bottom plank on the body and another small parallel line to indicate the tip of the hooves of the missing legs. Now it is a case of freehand drawing the new leg between these two marks. The shaping of the leg will be similar to the other pair in size and width, but the knee or hock will be different; back hooves are kicking back and front hooves are pointing down, as if on the front tip of the hoof. The knees and hocks should be parallel, that is, between knee or hock and body is the same length on front and back legs, as is hoof to knee

or hock and the stride of the horse should be made so that the body is central and the legs are out as much at the back as they are at the front. Photographs of rocking horses are a great help for this. The size and shape of the tenon can be measured from the horse itself. If your drawings are exactly the same size as an original leg, cut just outside the drawn lines when cutting out on the band-saw, to allow for sanding off at a later stage and make the tenon slightly oversized; it is easier to make it smaller, if need be, than try to pack out an undersized one.

Carve the leg with a chisel or spokeshave in the same manner as the original one, finishing with coarse, then fine sanding discs on a hand-held drill, followed by hand sanding. The shoulder at the top of the leg is cut on a slope; saw this out and the thickness of the tenon. Both shoulder and tenon should be checked with the mortice in the body and not the old leg, in case this was a mismatch; the shoulder will be only on the outside of the leg, while the tenon and inside top of the leg are on the same plane with no ridge between. When the tenon and shoulder are finished, fit the tenon into the mortice and put the whole horse on to the hoof rails or rockers to check that the leg is fitting correctly. Bear in mind that in most cases there will be a piece to cut out of the hoof of the new leg for the hoof to sit on the hoof rail or rocker perfectly. Therefore the new leg and its pair will either have to balance on top of the hoof rail or rocker, or be propped into position. Very old horses on rockers did not have the hooves cut away; the bolts alone took all the weight of the horse as the hooves were bolted to the sides of the rockers, so this type will need careful propping to get the leg in the right position. When satisfied that the new leg is in the correct position, take it off, making sure that the areas to be glued are free of dirt, dust and old gesso. Smear the tenon and shoulder with glue, put in the mortice and put the horse back on its hoof rails or rockers, propped if necessary, and leave to dry where it won't be disturbed. To give extra strength, when dry, put in dowels as described in the section marked leg joint.

To put the rebate in the hoof, if it is needed, stand the horse with its old hoof of the pair on a block, the other pair in their right place and new toe tips on the rocker or hoof rail. Measure up the hoof the same distance on the new one as shows on the old to the top of the rebate and draw a line parallel to the hoof rail or rocker and carry this parallel line round the front and back of the hoof. Mark another line on the front and back of the hoof that is just wide enough to allow the hoof (when the rebate is cut out) to drop over the hoof rail or rocker without any slack. Saw out the section not required. The horse will now drop into its correct position. Give a final check that the swinger bars, if using a hoof rail, can swing freely between the legs and then the new bolt hole can be drilled in the hoof of the new leg.

Ears

The ears are very vulnerable to damage, because if the rocking horse is too near an object at the front, the ears are the first thing that comes into contact when the horse is in motion. If the damage is only slight chipping, either sand away the chipped part (many owners like their horses ears stunted like this) or fill in with wood filler. Greater damage, such as half an ear missing, a lost ear or both gone, will need some careful carving done on the replacement so that it matches the remain-

ing ear, or if both are missing the new ears need to be in keeping with the type of ear carved by the original craftsman.

In general late eighteenth- and early nineteenth-century horses had very small ears, average-sized ears by the mid-nineteenth century, slightly tall, well carved and elegant by the turn of the twentieth century, getting back to average sized around the 1920s to 1930s. Then in the 1960s still average sized, but not a great deal of shape. This is only an indication; individual horses that have been carved by an expert woodcarver will show his skill in the shaping of the ears, but for practical purposes when ears are very badly damaged these generalizations will help. For an ear that is half missing you can splice a new piece on as follows: plane or saw the broken surface flat. Cut out, in the same type of wood, a piece that is slightly bigger than the piece that is missing, being careful that the grain of the wood runs the same way as the rest of the ear. Screw and glue it into position and when dry remove the screw putting a small $\frac{1}{4}$in(6mm) dowel in its place. Carve the ear with a chisel, round surform, gouge and rifler file, then sand down to match the other ear.

If both ears are missing or badly damaged, saw a right-angled section out of the head from just behind the ears in a vertical line and just in front of the ears in a horizontal line. This will give the ears a solid base and make it easier to sit them correctly. Using a block of wood the same type as the head (usually pine) mark and cut out a slightly oversized pair of ears, making sure that the grain of the wood is along the length of the ears to give them maximum strength. Cut out the divide between the ears and do as much carving as possible before the ears are set into place, but still leave them slightly oversized just in case, when gluing them into place, there is any variation in the final position of the new wood. Glue and screw into place, the line of the screw being made central so that there is even pressure on the whole of the join. When dry remove the screw and replace with a ¼in(6mm) wood dowel. The ears are now ready to pare down to correspond with the surrounding wood exactly and have their height checked. Tidy between the ears with a rifler file, a final sand and the horse is ready for the next stage of gesso or paint.

Broken Jaw

If the jaw is so badly cracked that there is movement when the two sides of the crack are pulled apart, then the jaw will have to come off for glue to be put on the broken surfaces. Drill a screw guide hole in first before removing the jaw, screw the correct length of screw to be used into the wood so that you can see how the jaw will fit together eventually. This ensures that the screw is correctly placed, which will make it much easier to get the jaw to go back to its original position than drilling the hole afterwards and then trying to get two slippery, sticky surfaces to make contact correctly. Remove the screw and take the jaw apart, being careful to keep the broken surfaces clean. If it is the second time a repair is being done, remove dirt, old gesso and old glue, which can either be brushed or gently scraped away without taking the wood away with the glue, or as a last resort, gently scrub the surfaces with hot water but *do not soak*. Allow them time to dry thoroughly.

All the while try to keep the lines of the wood grain staying in their right positions and cut away any wood sticking up around the screw holes; this all helps to make a perfect mend. When the broken surfaces are clean, dust free and dry, smear with glue and screw the jaw into position, wiping away surplus glue. Withdraw the screw when the glue is dry and replace, depending on the size of the jaw, with a ¼in(6mm) or a ⅜in(9mm) wood dowel.

With a jaw that has been broken and unsuccessfully repaired, look for any screws, or less likely, nails. Treat the broken surfaces as above and glue into position. With this type of repair, very often part of the break does not match properly and there is a gap left, or there is a piece missing. Wait until the part that does match is dry and the dowel in place, then saw a wedge shape where the gap is and glue in an appropriate sized piece of the same type of wood. When dry sand to match the rest of the jaw.

Missing Jaw and Nose

The most difficult repair is when the jaw or jaw and nose are completely missing. The same procedure is used for either so the instructions here are for a missing jaw and nose which will be referred to as the 'nose'. First make the broken edge perfectly flat so that there is a good surface on which to fix the new nose. Next draw on a piece of hardboard or cardboard a profile of the nose you think should fit the horse. Cut it out and try it in position; two or three tries are usually needed before a suitable shape is decided upon.

Note: The original nose would have been cut out of the same piece of wood as the neck and the rest of the head of the horse, so the nose will not be longer than a line parallel with the bottom edge of the neck. The lips are usually drawn back to show the teeth so the back corners (which are rounded) of the mouth go back further than the nostrils. The nostrils are not quite on the end of the nose; there has to be room for a top lip. Don't forget the little chin under the bottom lip.

Mark the profile on a right-sized piece and type of wood, keeping the grain of the wood in the same direction as that to which the nose will be attached. Cut it out slightly larger, both in width and depth, but not length; the width should be as wide as the horse is across the eyebrows as the nostrils will be flared. Try it in place and if not satisfied have another go. Only small pieces of wood are involved so the cost is really only in time, but it is worth getting it right as the head is the most important feature of the horse. There is a choice at this point of doing most of the

> **Tip** If the gap in the jaw repair is under the chin somewhere and an ordinary saw is too big to use, try using a hacksaw, turning the teeth of the blade inwards towards the frame. Then in many cases the frame can be slipped over the nose and the flat surfaces, which are needed for a good join, sawn.

carving before gluing into place, perhaps wiser if you are not sure what the outcome of the carving might be, so it would be easier to start again or on the other hand carve *in situ*, in which case under the chin

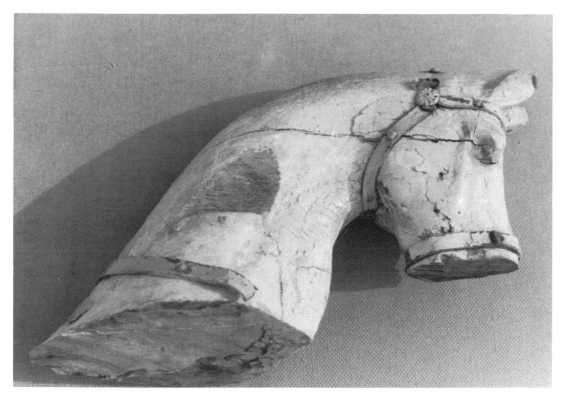

Half a neck muscle overlay, with eye and nose missing. One large crack.

carving can be difficult if the rest of the head is still attached to the horse. As horses only have four teeth each side, top and bottom at the front of their mouths, these will be the only ones showing (old makers were very particular about keeping to this) therefore there is a 3⁄16in(4mm) deep tenon-saw cut around the top and bottom lip to be chiselled away to form the teeth. It does not reach right to the back of the mouth. Length of teeth depends on size of horse. Nostrils should be fully flared, which means the round end with the centre carved out is almost sideways on to the bridge of the nose. There should be a sharp inward curve from the end of the nostrils back to the top lip and the rest of the face. The mouth itself would be quite narrow compared with the width between the tips of the nostrils. Leave the newly carved nose slightly oversized to allow for sanding and any discrepancy, if the nose is carved before gluing in place.

Use two screws for keeping a nose in place when gluing (one for a jaw only and use either 1⁄4in(6mm) or 3⁄8in(9mm) dowels when replacing the screws, depending on the size of the nose.

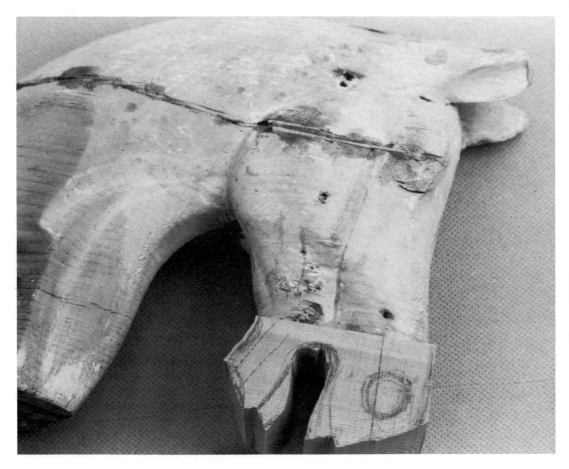

Slivers of wood glued into the crack. The oversized new nose glued on.

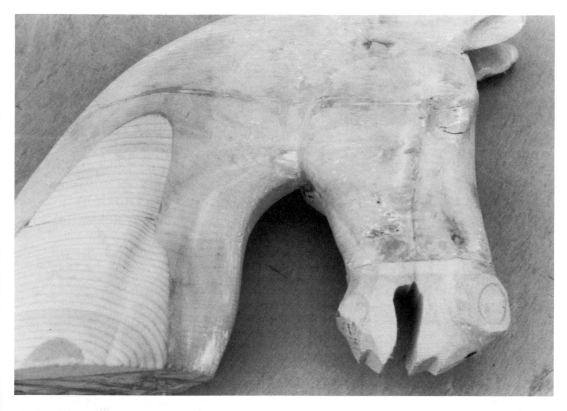

The finished nose, after carving.

Broken Head

Proceed as for a broken jaw. If it is a previous repair that has broken out again you might have to do a good deal of detective work to find all the nails and screws that have been used before. This is where past restorers very often excelled themselves in the number of things they used to hold the two sides together.

Eyes

Before 1940 the rocking horse eyes were made of clear glass with a black pupil in the centre and the back of the eye painted brown. This brown very often peeled away, even though the eye had not been

Tip When gluing, screwing and dowelling a piece of wood that has broken off back into position, drill the screw hole starting from the centre of the broken side of the wood being replaced, then drill outward to the outside surface. This disturbs the lines of the grain of the wood the least and you have the drill hole in the exact location where the screw will keep the two halves together correctly while the two pieces of wood are gluing together. This procedure is also good when putting a new nose or jaw on.

disturbed. In such cases if the eye is secure, leave well alone as they would have been set in gesso. Since about 1940 the eyes have had the brown colour in the actual glass which makes them look more alive and if the light is right they sparkle and glow. It is not quite the same with plastic eyes which are also available. One or two rocking horse manufacturers used a plated fancy headed domed nail instead of a glass eye, which would go rusty in time. Loose eyes should be reset and cracked eyes replaced for safety reasons.

To fit new eyes, clean out all old bits of gesso and dust from the eye socket. Fill the socket with wood filler (or as second best thick gesso) and press the new eye into position. Depending on the consistency of the filler the eye might have to be held in position for a minute or so until the filler has set. Smooth away any surplus filler and when dry, sand around the eye until smooth. This gives the round eye favoured in the past. The stylized painting of the eyes is given under painting section.

Muscles

A crack in the neck or top of the leg muscles (overlays) can be repaired by cleaning out dirt or sawing out the crack line the width of the saw and putting in a sliver of glue-covered wood.

There is always a reason for loose muscles such as the damp getting in and the pin nails that hold them having rusted away, the wood underneath not being quite flat or the muscles themselves being warped. With some muscles that only have one edge that has come away (usually the thin edge) the gap can be cleaned out and slivers of like wood, covered in glue inserted and sanded to match when the glue is dry later. Very loose ones can be taken

off and the surface planed flat (beware of hidden pin nails) and reglued on, but many are too bad to save or are missing. Keep even the worst ones until the repair is complete before getting rid of them; they may be useful to refer to. To do a replacement, cut out a piece of like wood to the size and thickness of the thickest part required (*see* page 51). Check that the surface it is intended for is flat and clean, glue and clamp it into position. If the clamps won't reach or the piece of wood keeps slipping, screw it into position instead. Take the screw away when dry and fill the hole with wood filler. Chisel and sand down the surface to blend in with the rest of the horse. As there is no strain on any of these muscles it is not necessary to put a wooden fixing dowel through them.

Wooden Backrest

Except for very small rocking horses, all the old horses had wooden backrests to the saddles between the end of the eighteenth century to the early twentieth century and some horses still do. They were a flattened half moon shaped piece of wood that was inserted about ½in(13mm) to ¾in(18mm) deep across the back of the horse and at the back of the saddle, just in front of the hip (point of croup). It was about 1in (25mm) wide, flush with the horse's hips each side and curved up to between 1½in(38mm) to 2½in(63mm) centre back and held in position with two large screws or nails. It was made in the same wood as the body with the grain of the wood along the length of the backrest and not across the breadth. A new rest needs to be a snug fit and can be glued and dowelled into position with small dowels. The top edge of the backrest should be chamfered or bevelled so that it is parallel

with the ground. It is painted the same colour as the horse.

Stirrup-Strap Staples

Just below the pummel hole, if there is one (*see* Chapter 1) and about three-fifths of the way up the horse's ribs, towards the front of the saddle area on each side, there is often a part of the wood scooped away 1½in(38mm) ×¾in(19mm) ×½in(13mm) deep (these sizes vary a great deal with different horses). This area should have a metal bar across it on which to hang the stirrup-straps. The bars are often missing and need replacing by hammering a very wide U-shaped staple (for details on making the staples *see* 'Stirrup-Straps' in Chapter 5). Sometimes there is no area scooped away, just the U-shaped staple and sometimes there is nothing at all and no signs such as telltale round holes to show where the staples have been. In the latter case the stirrup-straps were fixed by other means.

Bow Rockers

These are comparatively maintenance free provided they are fitted correctly in the first place and are of wood free from blemishes. There should be between five and seven softwood bars each approximately 3in (76mm) wide by ½in(13mm) thick covering the box section in the centre. Often this has been replaced by a piece of plywood which is sufficient but not correct. Most rockers were painted a dark green in the nineteenth century, occasionally black or dark red with later ones clear varnished. The biggest problem with bow rockers is that children stand on the spacer bars at the ends to get a ride, when someone is already sitting

on the horse itself. This in time causes the bars to give way as the old spacer bars were held in place with two nails each side; the newer ones have screws.

In the past if the spacer bars came loose another few nails were banged home so in the end with all the rusting metal the spacers fell to bits. These spacer bars or turned ends were about 1½in(38mm) 1¾in(45mm) in diameter with plenty of grooves in the turnings that were not very deep. In replacing these it is one of the few cases where it is better to use large screws rather than dowels because children will stand on the ends and dowels cross break much more easily than screws. When the horse is off the rockers the sides of the rockers very often appear to be out of line. If they are working correctly and are sound, leave well alone as horse and rockers will have changed shape together over the years.

Sometimes the change in the rocker has loosened the leg that is bolted to it. In such cases a new alignment of the leg is needed, or if the condition is extreme, a new straight quarter section of rocker must be made and fitted. Insect infestation and rot are the two biggest enemies of rockers (see woodworm and rot) with cross breaks a poor third. Old cross breaks have usually been treated by screwing or bolting a section of wood across the break. This needs looking at very carefully to see if any movement has developed. If you have any doubts about the sound condition of the wood or its fixings then the whole section should be replaced; a weakness there and the whole rocker becomes unsafe to use.

Swinger Stands

These were not invented until the very late 1870s, but there is much more maintenance

needed with them than there is with a bow rocker, as there are moving parts that wear in time. The stands made of softwood planks and hardwood (beech) pillars and hoof rails could be painted any one of various colours, clear varnished or dark varnished. Names and patents and details should be left if possible, as these are part of the horse's pedigree. Before starting to restore a swinger stand, leave it for two weeks in a dry warm atmosphere, if there is any chance of it having been in a damp one. The pillars that seemed tight very often loosen in the dry, warm atmosphere as the stand dries out.

The first check with the stand is for insect infestation and rot (see woodworm and rot). It is very subject to both, as although the top was nicely painted or varnished, there was rarely any put on the wood underneath, so even if everything is in good condition at the moment, put on woodworm killer as a precaution and seal the wood against rot at the end of the

Pillars for swinger stands, made by (from left to right) Ayres; an amateur (with end butts too narrow); Triang and one made for Harrods by an unknown maker.

restoration. Sometimes if there is only a little woodworm in the stop at the end of the bottom plank, provided they are treated, they are better left than trying to tackle the rusty nails and screws. Other parts of the stand that have any amount of woodworm etc., really do need replacing.

Pillars

If the pillars are loose, knock off the top plank with a wooden mallet, putting an odd flat piece of wood under the top plank where you intend to hit it with the mallet so that no damage is done to the plank. When the plank is off, check the bottom stubs of the pillars, because if they have been turned on a lathe and it is a pre-1940, the stand and bottom stubs of the pillars will almost certainly have a wooden thread – unless the stand has been made by an amateur – (see left) in which case all that is needed to tighten them again is to give them a good hard twist; a strap wrench makes an excellent job of this. The top stub of the pillars will have a wedge of wood pushed into it.

Carefully saw, with a tenon-saw, the wedge out again, or if more convenient saw another wedge shape in the butt. The wedge shape must be sawn so that the cut will be across the wood grain of the top plank when it is put back and not along it, as when the wedge is hammered into the butt, the wood of the top plank is likely to split if it is the wrong way. Make the wedge slightly thicker than the shape in the butt out of an odd piece of wood of the same type as the pillar if possible (usually beech). The grain of the wood of the wedge should run along its length, not across or down towards the point or it will break up when hammered in. Smear glue on the

stubs and drop the top plank back into position, smear the wedges with glue and hammer home with a wooden mallet. Because the wedges are slightly larger than the shapes in the stubs they will force the two sides of the stubs apart, just enough to make a strong join with the top plank. Cut off any surplus wedge, leave to dry, then sand smooth. The same procedure is used for the bottom stubs if they have no wooden screw thread, in which case put all four wedges in at the same time so that they can all dry together undisturbed.

Hoof Rail

This is the length of wood 2in(50mm) to 3in(76mm) wide 1in(25mm) to 1½in (38mm) thick and a little longer than the stride of the horse, to which the hooves are bolted and the metal rods of the swinger bars go through. Most children use the hoof rail to stand on when mounting the rocking horse so do check for cross breaks; if there are any, renew the offending rail. The other trouble spots are where the iron rods of the swinger bars go through the rails. If only softwood has been used for the rails, the holes wear oval and the swinger bars slop badly. Even hardwood rails wear in time so that the hole becomes enlarged and the extra movement makes a timid rider feel unsafe.

There are different ways to cure the problem. The most drastic is to renew the rails altogether. A simpler way is to plug the holes with hardwood and redrill the size of the hole needed for the swinger bar. Putting a metal sleeve into the hole is another option, but this has to be done correctly because if it is just pushed in, the sleeve will start turning around with the movement of the bar, and start the wearing process all over again. An

incorrectly fitted sleeve could also work its way out of the hole and jam on the bend of the bar where the bar comes out of the inside of the hoof rail and it bends up towards the fixing on the top plank of the stand causing limited movement of the horse. First plug and redrill the hole to the right size if necessary. The sleeve needs to be slit along its length and one of the edges of the slit turned over outwards. A corresponding groove is made in the side of the hole right through the thickness of the hoof rail. Check to see if the sleeve and hole fit well together; they must be tight, but not forced enough to split the wood, and then hammer the sleeve home. Brass or copper pipe are best to make the sleeve from as they are not too hard to bend at the edges. The swinger bar should now fit in and move freely without rattling about.

Swinger Bars

These are the two irons, sometimes plated, occasionally brass rods that hang in an upside down U shape from the top plank and go through the hoof rails at the ends of the U. Their function is to take the weight of the horse and rider and give a controlled rocking motion to the horse. They are usually either ⅜in(9mm) or ½in(13mm) diameter, the length depending on the size of the horse. Originally they were almost always painted black. The checks to make are to see that the swinger bars are moving freely, that they are even and straight and the horse sits straight on the hoof rails when the horse is in motion. Also the parts that are across the top plank do not move off the top plank at one side. Any of these faults means that the rocking horse has either been knocked over at some time or has always been kept against a wall. In this case the riders have had to

mount the horse from the same side each time using the hoof rail as a step and the pull to one side each time has gradually bent the swinger bars out of true. Unless you are a skilled blacksmith it is easier to buy new swingers than to try and bend the old ones back. The two parts of each swinger that go into the hoof rail must be *exactly* parallel with the section that sits on the top plank and the sections that drop from the top plank (the long sides of the U) to the hoof rail must do so at exactly the same 112½°angle on each side.

To fix the swinger bar through the hoof rail, sometimes a washer is put on, on the outside where the bar protrudes from the hoof rail and then the end of the bar is peened over. This is the flattening on the end of the metal bar with a ball peen hammer to stop the washer coming off and releasing the end of the swinger bar. Simple, but the disadvantage of this method is that it can be more difficult to renew the hoof rails if required, as it depends upon there being enough room to cut off the swinger end and redo it when the new rail is in place. Another problem is unless there is a jig made to hold the rails and swinger bars steady, the swingers can be hammered out of line. The most common way of securing the swinger ends is to put the washer on the part of the bar that protrudes from the hoof rail and then keep washer and bar in place by putting a split pin through a small hole drilled in the end of the bar. This is then covered over with a metal cap for protection. Very often the caps are very battered because they are only thin pressed metal, or are missing altogether. Three tiny holes on the hoof rail around the swinger bar end will tell you if caps were used, as they were kept in place with three gimp pins. A cap of a hardwood block to match the hoof rail can be put over the ends for protection, but unless neatly turned on a lathe they usually look rather large and clumsy and new metal caps are available.

With most old horses there is wear where the swinger bars lay across the top plank. There should be a metal plate (base plate) fixed to the top plank and underneath the swinger bar. This is usually badly worn or missing altogether. It can be replaced with a 2½in(64mm) to 3½in (88mm) long metal strip ¼in(6mm) wide and ⅟₁₆in (1.5mm) thick, nailed in place with two gimp pins. Before nailing it, check that the edges of the plank are not worn down. It might be worth taking a little of the wood away with a chisel to make a flat surface and then building up to the right depth with new wood. The other check to make before nailing the metal strip down is to put the swinger bar in place on top of it and then screw and bolt the clamp over the bars to make sure that the swinger bars swing freely with no looseness. If it is tight or slack, adjust the depth of wood under the plate.

There is one more thing that might upset the balance of the swinger bars and that is if the top plank itself is crooked. To check this, have the plank at eye level and look from one end along the length towards the other end. A slight twist can be compensated for by having one end of the base plate deeper into the wood than the other, but this only works for a slight twist, otherwise a replacement top plank is needed.

Clamps

The last check to make on the swinger stand is to look at the clamps holding the swinger bars. Even quite sturdy ones can be bent or cracked. First lay them on a flat

surface and see if they sit perfectly flat; any wobble, or bent edges, and it is best to replace them as rattling at this point will undo any restoration you have done to other parts of the movement of the swinger bars. Good strong clamps with the swinger bars working correctly underneath will give a very smooth ride and confidence to the rider. Good reproduction clamps can be bought or details of how to make your own are found under 'clamps' in the chapter on making a medium rocking horse.

Mane

Up to the 1970s for nearly all rocking horses that had hair manes, makers used either a cow's, but more often a pony's tail for the mane. The cow or pony tail was cured with the long hair still attached to the leather. Strips about ½in(13mm) wide were cut, with a sharp knife, on the leather side of the tail. To replace the mane, remove any old mane that is left and more importantly remove as many of the old nails as possible. Most horses have had more than one mane as they are the first thing to wear out. Round any holes left from the nails, hook out crumbling wood that is affected with rust from the nails and fill the holes with wood filler. The strips of tail are now nailed with 1in(25mm) nails on to the ridge of the horse's neck or in a groove carved especially to take them, the heads of the nails being hidden amongst the hair. Butt one strip to the next strip, ending 2in(51mm) or 3in(76mm) above the saddle position. A further small piece of tail is turned with hair flowing in the opposite direction and nailed from the back and between the ears to form the forelock.

Other ways have now been devised to attach the hair. One favourite is to clip and glue loose horsehair between two 1in(25mm) wide pieces of leatherette and drop into a slot cut in the neck of the horse, nailed and glued into position. Another is to use the loose hair glued into the leatherette as before and just nail it onto the neck of the horse. The former way looks better but may mean altering the neck, the latter is a bit amateurish, but the best way of all for an *old* horse is with the tail as near to the original as possible. Nails are used to attach the mane as it makes it easier to lift off when it is worn out and replace.

Tail

About a 2in(50mm) piece of the pony tail used for the mane, usually the very end with the longest hair is made into a tail for the horse by tacking it to a wooden plug. The tail, like the mane, wears out with constant playing by children. A horse will usually arrive for restoration with no tail or plug or a firmly jammed plug with a few whisps of hair attached. If the tail plug is missing the tail hole invariably needs cleaning out. Rag, candle, crayons and string are all quite commonly found in tail holes. For a jammed tail plug which is only a piece of softwood, it is not worth taking much time to release as it is much easier to drill it out with a twist drill. There will be nails so it is a bit risky to use a chisel, or gouge. When the tail hole is clean, make a softwood plug about 2in(50mm) long, small enough to get the plug and the piece of tail which is wrapped round it into the tail hole by at least 1in(25mm) and to wedge there. Some of the very old horses had tapering tail holes. When satisfied that the tail will fit, tack the piece of tail around the plug with tacks, smear with glue and tap into place with a wooden mallet. Be careful not to make it so tight that the

wood around splits, but it must be tight enough not to be pulled out by exploring fingers.

An alternative method of making a tail is to glue and bind long loose horsehair around a small plug with a hole in the centre big enough to put a screw or nail through. When dry a screw or nail can be put through the hole in the centre, the plug and top of the hair smeared with glue and screwed or nailed securely into the tail hole. When using this method, if the tail hole is very deep, more than 1½in (38mm), glue a softwood plug in the bottom of the hole first so that there is a solid surface to which to screw or nail the tail.

Saddle

Before the 1920s all saddles were made of leather (usually ¹⁄₁₆in(2mm) cowhide) and the centre was padded with horsehair in the better quality horses and cotton waste in the ordinary ones. The 1920s and 30s saw the introduction of Rexine, which was a synthetic leather using cloth as a base. Rexine became popular as a cover for part, if not the whole saddle, and in the 1960s plastic-coated cloth (leather cloth) and corduroy appeared. Some of the old leather saddles were red, the colour fading away with age to brown, which was the colour of the majority. The Rexine covered saddles kept their colour better if they were red, but the synthetic covering cracked off. This also happens with the later plastic-covered ones. Leather is still the best for durability, especially if the riders are encouraged to use leather cleaning products from time to time.

It does not follow that because a horse has the remains of a Rexine saddle it was made in that period. Very few really old horses have their original trappings attached; if they have they are more use as museum pieces and should not be stripped. It is much more likely that if all other indications are of an earlier horse, the later saddle only indicates the last time the horse was restored.

The old saddles had a central padded area running from the base of the neck to the wooden backrest, the small front neck edge being parallel to the much longer back edge, which overlapped on to the top of the wooden backrest. The sides sloped outwards in straight lines from front to back. Sewn or nailed to these edges are two sets of flaps, in shape very similar to the flaps of a real saddle. The top flaps are small, but big enough to protect children's legs from stirrup-strap buckles. The under-flap is much larger and takes some of the wear off the horse that is caused by the movement of the stirrup-straps. Between these two flaps, on each side is a hole approximately ¾in(19mm) cut in the leather and through the wood of the horse underneath. The holes were for the pummels to be fitted into, when required. Just below the pummel holes another piece of leather is taken out to show the metal bar for the stirrup-straps to be hung upon. Brass domed nails were used to fix the saddle to the horse, along both straight sides of the padded area and around the edges of the larger, side flaps. Across the top of the wooden backrest a strip of leather, the same width as the backrest, was nailed on to hold the back edge of the padded saddle in place. The last nail at each end of this strip was usually a fancy brass rosette. Some of the later leather saddles had no top flap, but instead had a little shaped piece of leather nailed at one end that would cover the pummel hole when not in use (*see* right).

Old tack on an F.H. Ayres horse.

From the 1920s onwards there were no pummel holes. Some horses retained the metal bar for the stirrup-straps; others had a long strap that went over the back and screwed to the horse under the saddle with a stirrup at each end. The straps were not usually adjustable. Others just had the stirrup-strap nailed to the horse under the side flaps of the saddle. Both the last two options gradually wore with use and either had the nails pulled out that were holding the saddle flaps or the saddle flaps themselves torn.

Most of these saddles are worn away or missing completely. Sometimes a complete saddle, if of leather, can be saved by cleaning it well with saddle soap, but usually a complete new saddle is needed.

Pummel

Rocking horses originally had two pummels each for the girls to use to hook their legs over to ride side-saddle. They were about 6in(150mm) long and 1½in(38mm) wide, made of hardwood and curved like a banana. The inside curve was flat and the edges rounded; the outside curve could be either flat or rounded. At one end 1½in(38mm) of the wood was cut smaller, round and at an angle to the rest of the pummel; this stubb and the angle between it and the rest of the pummel varied a great deal from horse to horse. It had to slip easily into the pummel hole, but leave plenty of room between neck and pummel for the girl to hook her leg round it. Because of this angle great care needs to be taken when making a replacement, to ensure that the grain of the wood is as long as possible along the length of the pummel and stub. The pummel itself had matching leather to the saddle glued on, the join being at the side which was covered by a thin strip of leather going up one side over the top and down the other side, glued and

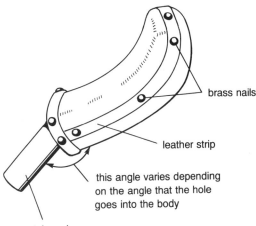

A leather-covered pummel.

nailed in place with brass domed nails. A similar strip of leather was glued and nailed round the bottom of the pummel. The stub was not covered with leather.

Crupper

A ½in(13mm) or ¾in(19mm), depending on the size of the horse, strip of leather using brass domed nails was nailed from the centre of the back of the horse behind the wooden backrest, down the horses' rump and around the tail looping round on to itself again, a representation of a crupper strap (*see* page 155, top).

The remains of red ribbon rosettes under fancy brass rosettes, used between 1880–1925.

Martingale

A ½in(13mm) or ¾in(19mm), to match the crupper strap, strip of leather using brass domed nails and sometimes small brass rosettes was looped and nailed around the base of the neck, ending in a V on the horses chest. From the point of the V a further strip of leather went between the centre of the forelegs, the end being nailed underneath, just out of sight. The centre of the V on the chest usually had a decoration such as a red ribbon rosette, a brass maker's name plate or a brass rosette (*see* below left). Rocking horse martingales like the crupper straps have no useful function at all; they are purely decorative.

Bridle and Reins

Bridles are made of ½in(13mm) wide leather and consist of a brow band, nose band, throat lash and a main head strap, all nailed in place with brass domed nails (*see* below left). The main head strap is looped round the ring of the bit and nailed in position, the next nail is halfway up the cheek, another being at the temple where the brow band and throat lash meet. The head strap then goes over the head behind the ears and covers up the join in the mane between the forelock and mane. The head strap then returns down the other side of the face to be looped round the ring of the bit at the other side of the mouth and again nailed securely. The reins will also be fixed to these two bit rings and the nose band of the bridle may be in two strips, one over the nose, above the nostrils, and have each end looped through the bit ring and secured (*see* page 31, top), the other piece going under the jaw and just behind the chin and also looped through the bit rings and secured. Alternatively the nose band may be in one piece and not go through the bit rings at all. The brow band is nailed across the forehead from one temple, under the forelock, to the other temple. The throat lash starts at the temple, goes in a curve round the jaw line next to the neck under the throat and up round the jaw again, back to the opposite temple.

Where the different strips of leather meet at the temple has always been a favourite spot for putting a ribbon rosette each side, or a brass rosette or both. The reins are made ½in(13mm), short in length so that a child will not sit too far back on the saddle when holding them. All the leather needs is to be checked for such things as splits and cracks. It is better to change the leather for new, rather than leave it to cause an accident, especially with the reins. The bridle described here is the design used on British horses. Horses made in other countries may have a different design.

Bit

Except for a few types in the 1930s and since 1960 the bit and the two rings attached were painted iron. The bit itself was about 1/16in(1.5mm) thick, stiff wire which went through the back of the mouth gap and was looped round a ring at each side of the mouth (*see* page 32). The rings often had two spikes with rounded ends attached, similar to a real horse's bit. They were painted black, so scraping off any rust and then painting with rustproof paint, followed by a coat of black paint, is all that is required.

Stirrups

There are two checks to make on the stirrups, which vary in size, depending on the size of the horse and also the rider for whom they were intended. Firstly make sure there are no cracks or breaks. The second thing that should be checked is that the stirrups are strong enough to do the job for which they were intended. Very often the original stirrups have been lost and very poor substitutes have been used instead.

Saddle Cloth

The saddle cloth was a piece of plain coloured material, nailed to the horse's sides, underneath the large saddle flaps. It was purely decorative as it had no function other than to be a pleasing colour and look similar to the numnah used on real horses. The early saddle cloths were made of a worsted wool cloth or felt, usually in blue or red with decorative braid or fringe around the edge. Sadly, all that usually remains is a few whisps of material under a brass domed nail. The shape would have been roughly oblong, the front edge curving outwards from the withers by the front of the saddle to the bottom front corner. The bottom edge was parallel with the floor and the bottom back corner elongated out to make it more stylish, a shape favoured for numnahs of the officers' cavalry horses during the nineteenth century.

Further decorations of brass rosettes and domed nails were sometimes nailed on to the saddle cloth. Red wool velvet became a favourite at one stage, later some horses had Rexine saddle cloths in red or brown and later still plastic leather-cloth ones appeared. Not all horses had these saddle cloths; to detect if they had, look for the tell-tale nail holes where the brass domed fixing nails had been (*see* overleaf).

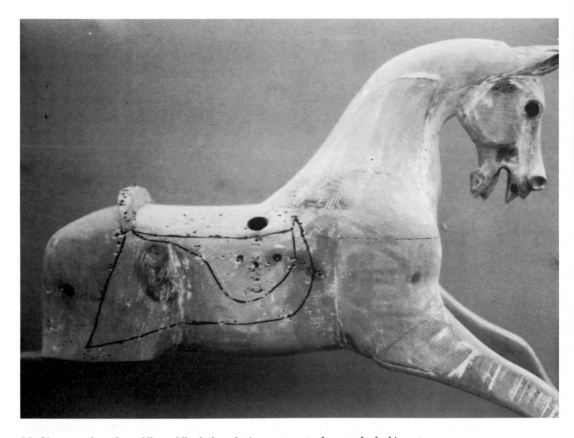

Marking out where the saddle, saddle cloth and stirrup strap staples were by looking at the nail holes.

OTHER DESIGNS

Around the turn of the twentieth century and onwards patents were taken out for numerous designs of stands for rocking horses. Many have not stood the test of time, but there are still some to be found and many of these use in their mechanism a piece or pieces of metal as a spring. These springs were subject to rust and metal fatigue so should be considered suspect until proved otherwise. Another design that is not 100 per cent wooden is the stuffed horse, the frame of which is only nailed together. The nails keep in perfect condition in the middle of the stuffing, but work loose and so need tightening. The old skin covering both wears out and shrinks. To get the hair going in the right direction all over the horse, two or three cured calf-hides, with summer length hair on them, are needed. Soak them for 24 hours in cold water to make them stretch and follow the contours of the horse, especially the face. Cut the skins to size on the body rather than try and take a pattern off the old skin. This is a hand sewing job. Remember the skin will shrink when it dries.

CHAPTER ELEVEN

TAIL PIECE

The value of rocking horses has been steadily rising in real terms since the 1970s and shows no signs of stopping as yet. The price a horse can command depends on many factors, including its age, condition, the rarity and quality of its make, and any unusual features it may have.

Few of the old makers put any indication on their horses as to who made them, but some did, such as the brass medallion with a thistle in the centre, introduced in 1910 by G & J Lines Ltd of Caledonia Street, London and their successors using a circular green disc with a red triangle on it for the firm Triang, changing this to a triangular plate in 1927. Another example is the signature of F. H. Ayres of London. These makers' names should not be mistaken for stamped marking and sometimes plaques that appear on the swinger stands of some horses indicating the shop for which the horse had been especially made, e.g. Harrods, London. The stamp mark of a patent number and date may also appear on the stand. This is not necessarily the date when the horse was actually made, as patents last for five years and providing the payment is made when due, can run for many years. Other little indications of a maker may be found, for instance, LB stamped on the stand clamps refer to Lines Bros. and both Ayers and

Triang had a distinctive pattern of pillars. Triang also had a wood plug in the top of the head of their horses. If an approximate date is known (indications of which are described in the chapter on history, with some further small details in the chapter on restoring) or a maker's name, there is more interest and the price will be higher.

Size is important; very large horses and very small horses are not sought after so much as medium sizes. How fine the carving has been done, especially on the head, is very important and only second to the condition of the horse. Time of year has an effect on the price too; nearing Christmas time is a seller's market.

In 1968, the British Post Office used a rocking horse for the design of their 4p Christmas stamp. This stamp showed two children playing with a large bow rocker and was sent out on millions of envelopes. One can be sure that some of the Christmas cards they contained featured rocking horses as did displays in toy shops up and down the country.

Let us hope that the children who received the cards, or stood outside the toy shops, gazing open-mouthed in wonder and excitement, will one day receive a rocking horse, for it still remains one of the world's most loved toys and companions.

INDEX

Italic numerals denote page numbers of illustrations.

accessories, 24–35
appaloosa, 7, 70
Ayres, F.H., 150, 155, 159

backrest, 134, 148–9
barrel horse, 5–6
bit, 6, 32, 33, 157
body, 14, 15
bridles, 6, 30, 156–7

centre of gravity, 15, 16
clamp, 16, 64–5, 152–3
cracks, 139
cross plank, 61
crupper, 29, 156

dappling, 69–70
design, 15
doll-sized rocking horse, 74–82
dowel, 16–17
dry rot, 135, 138

ears, 143–4
eyes, 7, 8, 12, 147–8

fibreglass, 11
finishes, 65–71
fur fabric, 12, 79

galloper, 159
gesso, 8, 18, 66–8, 134, 137
girth straps, 30
glue, 17, 138

heads, 7, 8, 11, 15
history, 5–12
hoof rail, 14, 15, 16, 62–4, 151

jibber, 7, 40

large rocking horse
    on rockers, 122–33
    on swinger stand, 110–21
Line Bros., 9–10, 159

mane, 7, 8, 33–5, 153
martingale, 29, 156
Mayhew, Andrew, 7, 18
medium rocking horse, 37–73
    accessories, 39
    alternatives, 48–9
    body carving, 44–8
    dimensions, 37

ears, 42
eyes
    carved, 43–4
    glass, 55–7
    plastic, 55–7
finishes, 65–71
head
    carving, 40–2
    construction, 39–40
    design, 40
legs, 49–53
materials, 38
neck, 44
nose, 42
pattern, 72–3
rockers, 57–9
swinger stand, 59–65
time, 38
tools, 38
mortice, 7–8, 50, 140–2

nails, 16–17, 139–40
numnah, 29

painting, 68–71
pillars, 9, 14, 16, 61–2, 150–1
plywood, 11, 74–82
points of a horse, 13
pummel, 7, 10, 134, 138–9, 155–6

racer, 7, 40
reins, 33, 156–7
restorations, 134–58
    backrest, 148
    bit, 32, 157
    bridle, 156
    crupper, 156
    ears, 143–4
    eyes, 147–8
    gesso, 137
    head, 147
    jaw, 144–6
    leg, 140–3
    mane, 153
    martingale, 156
    muscles, 148
    paint, 137
    reins, 156–7
rockers, 149

boat shaped, 9, 66, 122, 126–9,
    134, 149
bow, 8, 11, 12, 15, 57–9
rocking horses
    details
        saddle, 154–5
        saddle cloth, 157
        stirrups, 157
        swinger stand, 149–53
    doll size, 74–82
    large horse on rockers, 122–33
    large horse on swinger stand,
        110–21
    medium, 37–73
    small lightly carved, 83–94
    stuffed, 12, 158
    toddler's, 95–109

saddle, 154–5
    carved, 27
    cloth, 157
    removable, 27–8
    side saddle, 7, 10, 11, 134, 139
    simple, 24–6, 28
    traditional, 25–7, 154–5
screws, 16–17, 139–40
small, lightly carved rocking horse,
    83–94
space bars, 17, 128, 134, 149
springs, 158
stripping, 138
stirrup strap, 28
    staples, 28
stirrups, 33, 157
stuffed rocking horse, 12, 158
swinger
    bars, 16, 63–4, 151–2
    stand, 9, 12, 18, 59–65, 149–50

tails, 7, 8, 35, 153–4
tenon, 7–8, 50, 140–2
toddler's rocking horse, 95–109
tools, 7, 19–23, 24
Triang, 150, 159

varnish, 69, 134

wet rot, 135, 138
wood, 13–15
woodworm, 136-7